Counselling People with Communication Problems

Counselling in Practice

Series editor: Windy Dryden
Associate editor: E. Thomas Dowd

Counselling in Practice is a series of books developed especially for counsellors and students of counselling which provides practical, accessible guidelines for dealing with clients with specific, but very common, problems.

Counselling People with Communication Problems

Peggy Dalton

SAGE Publications
London • Thousand Oaks • New Delhi

© Peggy Dalton 1994

First published 1994

Sage Publications Ltd
6 Bonhill Street
London EC2A 4PU

Sage Publications Inc
2455 Teller Road
Thousand Oaks, California 91320

Sage Publications India Pvt Ltd
32, M-Block Market
Greater Kailash – I
New Delhi 110 048

British Library Cataloguing in Publication Data

Dalton, Peggy
  Counselling People with Communication
  Problems. – (Counselling in Practice)
  I. Title II. Series
  362.4

  ISBN 0–8039–8894–x
  ISBN 0–8039–8895–8 (pbk)

Library of Congress catalog card number 93-087620

Typeset by Mayhew Typesetting, Rhayader, Powys
Printed in Great Britain by Biddles Ltd, Guildford, Surrey

Contents

Acknowledgement

My special thanks to The Wednesday People, whose encouragement has kept me going through the writing of this book and whose shared experience of working with people with communication problems is reflected in its pages.

Preface

The term 'communication problem' may quite reasonably be applied to a vast range of difficulties, from the electronic to the deeply psychological. It is necessary therefore to begin by specifying the areas of concern to be addressed in this book and the reasons behind their selection. As a speech and language therapist for many years, my work has been with children and adults who have a difficulty with speech, language or voice, due to developmental delay or malfunction or acquired disorder of organic or psychogenic origin. It was the growing sense of the psychological needs of such people that led me, along with colleagues, to seek training in counselling. And although I have since worked with many who find interpersonal communication difficult for other reasons, here the focus will be on those particular client groups that came within my original sphere of work.

Selecting the problems

In the first outline of this book three very important areas involving communication problems were included: hearing impairment, learning difficulties (or mental handicap) and autism. On reflection, however, it was felt that the range and complexity of problems within all of these areas warranted a separate volume for each. And they deserved a specialist author with rich experience in these fields. With great reluctance, too, group work has been excluded, although psychological difficulties can be addressed very effectively in such a context (see Fawcus, 1992, for an excellent overview). Individual counselling and work with family members are, however, the focus of this volume.

This left stuttering (itself not a unitary disorder), the many speech and language difficulties of children sometimes occurring alongside physical disability, problems with voice at all ages and the speech and language disorders acquired through brain damage in later life. It is not possible to exemplify counselling work in all of these situations. But there are certain recurring themes of difficulty of development or adjustment which come with communication problems of all kinds: problems with self-concepts, with the expression of emotions and with social relationships in the young; those of loss of self, disturbed relationships, anxiety and depression in older people. The particular examples given of work with a number of people will, it is hoped, suggest the range and relevance of counselling for many more.

Choosing the language

I hope that these chapters will be of particular interest to speech and language therapists, to counsellors and to all who are concerned with human communication. But this poses a problem of language. Like most professions, speech and language therapy has its own set of diagnostic labels – a shorthand for those with a similar training background; a bit of a mystery for those without. I therefore decided that, at the risk of being old-fashioned (though not, I hope, politically incorrect) I would use as few speech pathology terms as possible and only those which are self-explanatory. I have, therefore, chosen to write of 'articulation problems' rather than 'phonological disorders', for example, and to describe someone as having difficulty processing language, rather than as having a 'semantic pragmatic disorder'. Only the general terms 'dysphasia' (for neurologically-based language disorders), 'dysarthria' (for neurologically-based articulation impairment) and 'dysphonia' (for voice problems) seem concise enough to include.

Aproaches to counselling

I have sometimes been asked which approaches to counselling are especially suitable for people with communication problems. As we shall see, however, these clients may be subject to all the psychological difficulties that trouble the rest of us and their speech, language or voice disorders may be the focus of their distress but not necessarily the main cause. The choice of approach, therefore, should be governed by their overall need and, principally, their own inclination. Psychological work which totally ignores the communication aspect would not, in most cases, be appropriate. Equally, counselling which never goes beyond it is likely to be limited in its effectiveness.

Reference is made to a range of interventions but a number of them recur in the literature. Personal construct psychology is perhaps the most widely used. But cognitive behaviour therapy, Rogerian counselling and other client-centred approaches are also practised. For all their differences, which will be touched on, what these have in common is a focus on the person and concern for the client's present and future situation, with the past explored where it has a limiting influence on current choices and stances towards life.

The aim of this book

All the volumes in this *Counselling in Practice* series have their focus on a particular area of difficulty or a particular aspect of the counselling process. Here I hope to show how counselling may explore and help to alleviate the special problems experienced by those whose ability to communicate is in some way impaired. The psychological effects of such impairments are not widely understood. If they are made clearer through the following chapters and clients themselves and those involved with them, professionally or personally, are helped in some way to ease them, the purpose of this writing will have been served.

Peggy Dalton

1

Introduction: the People, the Problems

This first chapter highlights the importance of communication as an aspect of human development. The effects of impairment on the child's growth and on the older person's sense of self are described and the need for psychological as well as direct intervention discussed. In exploring the involvement of parents and other members of an adult's family, their needs are also considered. A review of the literature follows, surveying the evidence of the use of counselling in this area. And, finally, some suggestions are put forward as to the training needs of those working with communication problems.

Communication and personal development

The ability of human beings to develop language and communicate with one another through speech, as well as gesture, facial expression and body movement has been a source of fascination to philosophers, psychologists, linguists and all of us who reflect on those things which distinguish us from other species. Many have pointed out that spoken and written language are the media through which we learn to cooperate with one another and organize ourselves socially. Psychologists such as Luria and Yudovich also stress the fact that it enables us 'to represent the world to ourselves as we encounter it: and so to construct – moment by moment and year after year – a cumulative representation of "the world as I have known it"' (Britton, 1971: 7).

One of the greatest pleasures for many parents is to participate in their children's growing mastery of speech. Through their ability to understand and express themselves verbally children come to know what others think and feel and to communicate their own feelings and ideas to those around them. Confusions and misunderstandings do, of course, arise, but the potential is there for clarification in the normal run of things. As children develop and their world of people and experiences widens, spoken and written language become increasingly important. It is through the many forms of human communication that we are able to go beyond our immediate family situations and experiment with new ways of looking at things and consider new possibilities for ourselves.

When things go wrong

The natural development of communication in children may be hampered from the start. A baby born with severe brain damage, as in some cases of cerebral palsy, may never be able to understand or to speak, as well as suffering other disabilities of movement and perception. Others, with more specific damage, may show normal intelligence through some of their activities but be unable to process language (they are dysphasic) or unable to control and coordinate the muscles required for speaking (dysarthric or dyspraxic). Even where the difficulty is less severe, the subtle nuances of tone and inflexion will not be available to them. Social isolation is a potential danger, even where they are surrounded by a loving family. The psychological help available to the families of all these children may be as important as the care provided for the young people themselves.

Where there is failure to develop language or where speech is rendered unintelligible through neurological or other organic disorder, lack of verbal communication with others can have far-reaching effects on many aspects of a child's development. Reduced ability to comprehend and use language will hinder cognitive and social development and there is known to be a high incidence of emotional and behaviour problems among such children (Gordon, 1991). Conversely, emotional problems themselves may cause language delay, delay in the development of intelligible speech and dysfluency. At the extreme, a child may simply choose not to communicate, in cases of elective mutism, where silence seems to be the solution to an otherwise intolerable situation. A number of authors have suggested that many children may need to deal with the emotional issues before any progress can be made with speech, reading or writing.

Effects on the sense of self
There can be no doubt that communication problems may severely affect the development of self-concepts in the child. Early on, a sense of being loved and valued comes from the experience of being held, fed and kept warm, while neglect or harsh handling are the foundations for a poor self-image. Very soon, however, what is said to us or about us plays a large part in the

development of who we think we are. From comments on our behaviour, our ability to do things and our looks, reputations are set up within the family: for example, he is 'the slow one', 'the good boy', 'the cry-baby', or she is 'shy', 'a little mother', 'the fat one'. At the same time, children have dialogue with themselves and with others, some of which helps to define limitations, seeks to affirm achievements and asks for confirmation that they are worthwhile.

Where a child fails to develop adequate language, he or she will miss out on this aspect of self-definition. And even with language intact but limited speech, the inability to negotiate with others verbally, to stake one's claim to attributes that others are ignoring, or to deny an attribution that seems unfair, for example, means that the elaboration of self-concepts is impeded. By secondary school age, fifteen such children were assessed as having:

Poor self-/other-awareness,
Poor self-esteem/self-confidence,
Fear of failure,
Disruptive behaviour,
Inability to appreciate lingustic aspects of humour,
Avoidance of social situations,
Difficulty expressing emotions in socially acceptable ways,
Few friendships – low appreciation of what a 'friend' is or of how
    to go about making friendships (Rinaldi, 1991).

Adults who have experienced these difficulties as children can sometimes look back and see how being regarded as 'stupid' by a parent or a teacher has continued to affect their view of themselves, even with proof of ability from considerable achievement. The reactions of other children play a large part too. One study (Hall, 1991) shows that even with mild articulatory errors, young people were judged more negatively by their classmates than those without errors, in terms of their ability to communicate, their status as peers and how they would develop as teenagers.

There have been a number of studies which exemplify the negative stereotyping of children who stutter and dysfluency is perhaps the communication problem which is most often recognized as having psychological implications. The complex cause-and-effect issues related to stuttering will be considered more fully in Chapter 7. Suffice it to say, at this point, that extreme anxiety in the anticipation of speech failure may cause young people to avoid situations to such an extent that they become social isolates. Since speech is involved in much that they do, they (and others) doubt their abilities in many respects. If no help is given, low expectations may be carried into their working and later social lives.

Less common, though as potentially open to negative reactions and damaging to the person's sense of self are mutational voice disorders in young males, where the voice fails to mature. Teasing, even bullying, are all too common and a young person would need a great deal more self-confidence than most adolescents possess to withstand them. Doubts, in particular, about his sexuality may cause him much anguish. Although there are conflicting theories as to the causes of a failure to develop adult voice, many see the problem as largely psychogenic in origin (e.g. Hammarberg, 1987). But even where hormonal deficiency is found to be present and correctable, help is often needed to adjust psychologically to the new, low, unfamiliar voice which may then be developed.

Children and adults with a cleft palate or one which is inefficient in making a closure between the nasal air passages and the mouth may produce not only hypernasal voice but have some difficulty with articulation. Although operational procedures have improved greatly, it is not always possible to solve the problem surgically. Where malformation of the lip is also involved these people have a double burden of sensitivity to bear about how they sound and how they look. Cleft-palate speech and stuttering are the two disorders most often mocked in the media, with implications for the former of low intelligence. Young people may suffer deeply and unless attention is paid to the psychological implications both of their condition and of any attempts to alleviate it through surgery, they may establish patterns of negative self-perception which will be even more difficult to change as adults.

Young people who sustain head injuries may suffer severe loss of self-esteem together with the communication problems commonly involved. From active, gregarious lives, they may be reduced to greatly restricted mobility and a position of deeply frustrating dependency. One study (Monast and Burke, 1985) highlights the effects of damaged body image, fears of rejection and loss of ability to communicate on adolescent sexuality. Green (1986: 2) describes a group of young men referred to him and his colleagues because of 'sexual misconduct, poor school adjustment and delinquent activities'. They had very different priorities. 'Their preoccupation', he says, 'was with the impact their head-injuries had had on their independence, their sexual attractiveness, their job prospects, their popularity with mates, their mood and even their very personality. Their desire was not so much to be controlled as to be understood.'

The need for counselling communicatively impaired children

Children are referred for counselling for many different reasons – because they are troubled in themselves and because they trouble others. Young people can have difficulties in controlling their emotions or in expressing them. They may find it hard to relate to others or to make sense of themselves. Some children are traumatized by their parents' splitting up or by the loss of someone close to them. They may be physically, sexually and psychologically abused. Maladjustment or delinquency can spring from any of these experiences or seem to develop from unknown sources. Although many survive under great pressure and thrive with remarkable resilience, others are deeply vulnerable and need help if they are to fulfil a richer potential.

Children with communication problems are subject to all the vicissitudes referred to above and with inadequate language, unintelligible speech, malfunctioning voice or disruption in fluency may be even more liable to react adversely to these vicissitudes. Many children find it hard to express their feelings of bereavement. Some of these do not even have the opportunity to try. Frustrations over relationships or personal failure may be eased in many by talking. For some of these young people physical violence or withdrawal may be the only means of dealing with them.

Not being able to hold their own verbally they may also be more open to misunderstanding, neglect or outright abuse. The majority of families with children hampered in these ways are caring and concerned. Others, however, where the pressures on older siblings and parents may also be great, show no understanding of the children's situation and reject them as a hindrance or worse. Much has appeared recently in the media about the abuse of young people with learning difficulties and physical handicaps. This group of children is known to be subject to teasing and bullying and it is likely that their problems too are taken advantage of to the same extent in some situations.

Some parents and professionals involved with communicatively impaired children are very sensitive to their psychological as well as their educational and social needs. Others (as we shall see in Chapter 3) are focused on communication alone and look to remedial measures to bring them into line with their siblings. It may demand great ingenuity on the part of a counsellor to find ways of getting in touch with the feelings of such a child and to be able to see things as they do. But unless, in some instances, this is attempted, efforts to improve communication skills will be fruitless.

The needs of the family

As mentioned earlier, the parents and others who care for children with communication problems are often in great need of help and support. Where such problems are part of a wider physical disability it is recognized that coming to terms with having a handicapped child and adjusting life to his or her needs may be an enormous drain on the family, however compassionate its members may be. A number of associations, such as the Spastics Society, provide information and advice and many families become involved in self-help networks. Sometimes, however, parents or siblings may have great difficulty in dealing with the situation, with the anger and the guilt they experience, and seek counselling for themselves.

Where a child's problems are less severe there may, nevertheless, be tensions in the household, with a partner or another child feeling neglected and resentful. Such feelings do not always come to light so clearly and may emerge only in the context of seeking treatment for the child. As we shall see in Chapter 3, it may not be easy for the rest of the family to acknowledge the extent of their involvement. By focusing on the child's dysfluency or failure to develop speech, relationship difficulties may be ignored. It may be the speech and language therapist who helps the family members to recognize their own needs.

Communication problems acquired in adult life

Adults may suffer a gradual loss of the ability to communicate through illnesses such as Parkinson's disease, multiple sclerosis, or motor neurone disease. The experience of losing control, competency and independence is devastating and may be met by fierce denial or helplessness. For most there will be anxiety about the future for themselves and for others they are responsible for together with periods of depression and despair. With many physical and psychological changes to deal with, loss of speech may not always be the most obviously painful. But many people with such conditions suffer humiliation from the slurring of speech which so often occurs (dysarthria), giving the impression of reduced intelligence – for example, one client refused to converse with anyone she did not know having been accused of being drunk.

Much will depend, of course, on the person's sense of self before the illness and much too on the strength of their relationships with those close to them. Many manage with impressive dignity to adapt to changes as they occur, planning for the future of spouse and children while there is time. Very often the counselling help sought by these people and their families comes through the associations set up for particular conditions, from others who are themselves involved in similar experiences.

The psychological effects of brain damage through strokes, tumours or cerebral infections may be even more shattering, in that they are usually sudden and unexpected. Where these involve loss of speech and language, initial confusion may be terrifying. Unable to understand explanations of what has happened and unable to ask questions, some people have reported later that they thought they had gone mad. As some degree of recovery often occurs quite soon, the terror may subside, but the full extent of more permanent impairment may take a long time for the people themselves and their families to grasp.

When this happens, just as the young head-injured people referred to earlier have to mourn the selves they might have become, older people may grieve deeply for the selves they were and the loss of all that they have built up in their lives. Many people develop a strong sense of who they are through work and now, especially where communication is severely affected, it is no longer possible for them to continue. Relationships change within the family, where interdependencies shift and one person may have to take on unaccustomed responsibilities, while the other feels useless and frustrated. The inability to discuss these things and to express feelings make such changes all the harder to adjust to.

Rehabilitation work with those who have suffered brain damage is usually focused largely on physiotherapy, occupational therapy and speech and language therapy to restore function. 'Counselling' is taken for granted as part of such treatments but it tends to be of the reassurance, advice and information-giving kind. This is often of great value in itself but lacking the emphasis on the client's feelings and views of the situation, which we associate with the term as understood by writers in this series. However, this is not to say that there is lack of sympathy or concern. Also, the difficulties of communicating on a psychological level in many cases has to be acknowledged. But, on the whole, especially with severe language impairment, it is the relatives who are listened to.

Language function is not affected where cancer of the larynx leads to laryngectomy. But there is often intense anxiety involved in the realization of the diagnosis itself and the experience of total loss of voice. Our voice is so much part of our identity that, without it, we feel diminished, unwhole. It is possible to learn to produce pseudovoice by activating the muscles of the oesophagus or to use various forms of artificial voice and other aids. Some achieve effective 'vocalization' by these means. Others, however, find them alien and choose to whisper or to write what they want to express. Either way, few would feel able to take part in social or work situations on equal terms with their fellows.

Not surprisingly, depression and anxiety are frequently experienced by people in this situation. When an alternative means of communication has been established, contact is often maintained with the therapist who worked with them through those early stages. There is a need to share the feelings of loss of potency and the fears of further illness with someone outside their immediate circle, perhaps. Other relationships may be changed by the event and reflecting on these changes in a counselling situation can help in coming to terms with them.

Other voice disorders among the adult population, although not life-threatening, may express quite severe levels of psychological distress. At one end of the spectrum there may be recurrent hoarseness or temporary voice loss signalling general fatigue and tension. At the other, longer-term loss of voice together with depression and/or anxiety may be one way of demonstrating that the person has reached the end of his or her tether and can only withdraw into silence. (No such assumption would be made, of course, without thorough investigation for possible organic factors.)

One screening of seventy-one patients with 'functional dysphonia', that is, huskiness or hoarseness of voice with no physical explanation, found little evidence of major psychiatric disorder (House and Andrews, 1987). However, eight had a past psychiatric history, two were said to have 'histrionic personality disorder' and twenty-two had clinically diagnosable mood disorders (primarily anxiety/tension states). Although work may simply be done to reduce undue tension and to facilitate appropriate breathing and use of voice, more often than not the psychosocial stressors preceding the onset of a period of functional dysphonia are discussed and attempts made to alleviate them.

Psychological intervention in work with communication problems

I have chosen the phrase 'psychological intervention' for this section because of the wide range of meaning implied by the term 'counselling' in the literature and the lack of distinction between it and 'psychotherapy'. It makes sense, therefore, to review how practioners have set about addressing the psychological aspects of communication problems first, and then attempt to define the nature of counselling in this context.

My search was not confined to books and journals relating to speech and language therapy, though it was inevitable that these formed the bulk of the five hundred or so references which emerged. Many of these were not useful, in that the 'counselling' included as part of a treatment programme was not described or seemed to be more in the nature of advice on how to implement the rest of the treatment programmes. The areas where psychological intervention is seen as an appropriate part of therapy are mainly speech and language problems in children with concomitant emotional and behavioural difficulties (e.g. Brooks, 1991), stuttering (see Chapter 7), head injury and other neurological trauma resulting in dysphasia (see Chapter 9) and some voice problems (see Chapter 8).

Although such intervention is mostly seen as running alongside direct work on language – for example, vocal rehabilitation or fluency – in some areas there is controversy as to whether a psychological approach alone should not be the focus of the work with clients. As will be shown in Chapter 7, treatments for stuttering have swung pendulum-like over the years between the extremes of those which regard dysfluency as the province of the psychotherapist or even the analyst and those who seek only to refine techniques and programmes for modification of speech behaviour.

In the late 1980s an American study (Hartman and Landau, 1987) comparing the progress of two groups of dysphasic clients, one undergoing formal language therapy and the other 'counseling', found that both approaches were equally effective in terms of language recovery. This brought protests from other clinicians (Albert and Helm-Estabrooks, 1988; Wertz, 1988) about 'methodological flaws' and 'errors in the literature review'. The efficacy of formal dysphasia therapy has been questioned repeatedly, the main difficulty being the measurement of the effects of a number of factors, such as the extent of the damage sustained, the phenomenon of spontaneous recovery, and social context. One element which does not seem to be addressed in these arguments is that of client choice. As we shall see in Chapter 9, some people in this situation see the restoration of language as their major goal and have no wish to share their feelings and fears. Others cannot work in a formal way and find attention to the emotional impact of their illness far more relevant. Against this, discussion as to which approach is the more efficacious becomes merely academic.

Counselling, in the study referred to above, is seen as 'emotional support for patient and family'. For young males with mutational voice disorders 'psychological counselling' was restricted to promoting 'acceptance of the low, unfamiliar voice' (Hammarberg, 1987: 204). For clients with functional dysphonia 'psychotherapy' is recommended, 'geared to the amelioration of presenting symptoms, rather than to the more lasting modification of the patient's character structure as in the more traditional psychodynamic approaches' (Canter, 1991: 13). In contrast, Nadell (1991) describes the use of existential psychotherapy with a 23-year-old man who had sustained a serious head injury, which involved addressing issues of death, isolation, meaninglessness and freedom in order to help him to create himself within the givens of existence. Streit (1988) similarly reaches beyond speech and language problems when she attempts to improve a child's 'psychic structuring' and help him with 'control of affect'.

A number of studies place emphasis on the psychosocial aspects of communication problems and provide family counselling. De Pompei and Zarski (1989: 78) describe their approach to the families of head-injured people who 'may be required to alter role allocation and reformulate family rules or else run the risk of stress overload and dysfunction'. Three family counselling strategies are used: educational counselling informs the members about cognitive–communicative disorders and promotes adaptive skills, family counselling addresses the emotional trauma of the head injury event and family therapy examines systemic functioning and conflict. Beery (1991: 163) stresses the importance of psychosocial and family influences as they relate to the vocal behaviour of adolescent boys with voice problems. He sees knowledge of the dynamics within the personal life and family of the adolescent as essential in understanding 'the etiology, maintenance and resolution of the dysphonia'.

Rustin (1987: 173) sees active parental involvement as essential when working with dysfluent children. Counselling sessions with parents not only address anxieties about the child's speech but extend, if appropriate, to other concerns within the family. For example: 'If there are marked relationship problems between the parents or if there are difficulties with other children in the family we try to ensure that the identified dysfluency problem does not divert attention away from these fundamental issues.' Hayhow and Levy (1989), in their work with young children who stutter, also see family interaction as having a profound effect on the development of communication skills. They advocate meeting the whole family in order to discover what significance the child's problem has for the different members and to observe patterns of interaction and the quality of communication, which may lead to identification of some of the causal and maintaining factors.

It will be seen from these few examples that the extent of psychological intervention varies greatly. Whatever it is termed, the focus of attention to the psychological aspects of communication problems ranges from attempts to enhance the efficacy of direct work on the specified difficulty, to the functioning of the person as a whole, to issues within the person's family environment. The nature and aims of the interventions are also varied, from emotionally supportive, to educational, to life-enhancing. And it is clear that any of these elements can be helpful in particular contexts.

A definition of counselling

What, then, will be the focus of this book on counselling people with communication problems? We may take it for granted, I hope, that anyone professionally involved with those affected in this way will be supportive, have some understanding of the implications of their difficulties and be prepared to acknowledge the intensity of feeling which may be experienced as they struggle to overcome them. All this is quite compatible with the diagnostic and intervention skills in which speech and language therapists are trained. These enable them to help children with their linguistic development, to prevent dysfluency and to alleviate it when it occurs, to undertake voice rehabilitation procedures and to work on the restoration of speech and language when these are affected in later life.

In many instances, however, it may be recognized that more is needed than a sympathetic handling of direct treatment procedures. The psychological impact of the communication problem may be such that attention to the person's anxiety, depression, lack of self-esteem and isolation is essential for any progress to be made with the communication skills themselves. Where parents and relatives are closely involved, their distress needs to be alleviated so that they are able to channel their emotional energy into the vital part they play in therapy. For this, other skills are needed in the therapist: listening for the clients' meanings and deeper feelings, helping clients to clarify the nature of their problems with themselves and in relationships with others, and assisting clients to discover their own resources for approaching life more effectively.

Training for counselling

In a chapter on personal construct psychology and speech therapy (Dalton, 1988) I bemoaned the lack of attention to counselling of any kind in the training of what were then called speech therapists. I acknowledged that things had improved somewhat over recent years, with students' attention being drawn more to the 'people' they were working with, rather than narrowly to the 'problems' they presented. Many qualified therapists were seeking post-graduate training in counselling at that time and this has increased in the intervening years.

In a survey of 244 therapists (Elias et al., 1989: 61) looking at the area of voice, most of them said that they undertook the treatment of psychogenic voice disorders. The therapists felt that the theoretical advice they had been given during their training was useful, but about a third of them had not had the opportunity of observing or treating such clients as students. As a whole they felt that they had acquired most of the psychological skills needed after qualification. The authors of the survey see a substantial need for post-qualification courses on work in this area and suggest that 'more practical instruction on psychological treatment might be incorporated in initial education'.

In a much smaller survey, but in relation to counselling in speech therapy as a whole, Miller (1990b: 3) found that all the respondents saw counselling as playing a part in the range of work they undertook. Some had had training in specific approaches to counselling, others described some particular skills they were conscious of employing. Most, she felt, 'indicated awareness of the client-centred nature of counselling'. When asked whether they had received any counselling training as undergraduates it was mainly those who had qualified within the previous five years who said that they had. But this varied from a one-day course to one day a week for three years and included 'sessions on social and communication skills', 'role-play sessions' and 'discussion groups'. Miller concludes: 'Explicit counselling theory seems to have been lacking in many of their undergradaute courses although several of the group had sought out courses to enhance their ability and develop specific knowledge once they were in practice' (1990b: 3).

It is not only in Britain that concern for the nature of psychological intervention with communication problems has been expressed. Chabot (1988), a Dutch author, discusses some common elements in different types of individual psychotherapy in the realm of speech therapy: the therapist–client relationship, client expectations, client attention and involvement and the therapist's conceptual framework. From Germany, Henze and Kiese (1990: 159) describe the functions and activities of what they term 'phoniatric psychology': 'a new clinical discipline that addresses the psychological dimensions of speech, hearing and language disorders'. They see the tasks of the phoniatric psychologist as involving 'psychodiagnosis, counseling, psychotherapy, training and supervision, and research related to communication disorders'.

Am I then saying that only those speech and language therapists with a thorough training in counselling 'should' become involved in the psychological aspects of communication problems? Clearly not. We have seen that there are many ways of giving psychological help to those affected as I have described. A sensitive understanding of the implications of communication impairment may be found among many professionals and carers involved and a number of associations provide invaluable support. What I am proposing is that clients who wish to go beyond the concerns of their particular difficulty, who seek to address the deeper issues of self-perception, relationship with others and their potential development, deserve to work with practitioners who have training and experience in both communication disorders and counselling.

There are some interesting accounts of practitioners from different disciplines working together with the same client. For example, Lockhart and Robertson (1977) (a speech therapist and a clinical psychologist), worked conjointly with people who stuttered, combining speech techniques and hypnosis. In a recent book on psychogenic voice disorders, Butcher (a clinical psychologist) and Elias and Raven (speech and language therapists) (Butcher et al., 1993), describe their treatment approach combining voice therapy and cognitive behaviour therapy. Cooperation with other disciplines, such as occupational therapy and physiotherapy is essential in many areas of communication work but in these two examples the work of the professionals is even more closely interwoven and needs to be jointly planned with great care.

Many psychotherapists and counsellors who are not also speech and language specialists work with people who have voice or fluency problems. A number of voice teachers have specialized in dysphonia related to stress or anxiety and combine their knowledge of voice functioning with psychological skills. Psychoanalysts, Adlerian therapists, personal construct therapists and others have taken a special interest in stuttering. And although dysfluency has attracted more than its share of charletons claiming magical 'cures', these professionals will have sought a wider understanding of this particular problem, whatever approach they then take to it.

Where there are language problems in child or adult clients, however, it does seem essential that anyone attempting counselling should also have trained as a speech and language therapist. As we shall see in Chapter 3, it is not easy to combine the listening skills of the therapist, 'analysing language for its content, form or use' and those of the counsellor, listening 'for the feelings behind what a person is trying to say' (Miller, 1990a: 2). But both are necessary in these instances. And where language or speech are greatly impaired the therapist's understanding of alternative means of communication may be crucial.

Summary

In this chapter I have attempted to give an overview of the kinds of difficulties which may be experienced by people with communication problems and the extent to which psychological intervention is currently practised. I have stressed the need for counselling training combined with an understanding of the communication problems themselves. Chapter 2 describes one particular approach to communication problems – personal construct psychology – which is widely used and would seem to be especially effective where changes in behaviour depend for their maintenance on changes in self-perception.

2

A Personal Construct Approach to Communication Problems

In Chapter 1 reference was made to a number of psychological approaches to communication problems. Here the focus will be on personal construct psychology (PCP). This is only partly because I have found it to be particularly useful for the assessment and management of the changes involved in these areas of difficulty. Kelly's ideas have undoubtedly contributed much to the development of counselling within speech and language therapy as a whole.

Some key features of personal construct psychology

It is only possible here to highlight some of the main features of construct theory. (A full account of PCP in relation to counselling is given in Fransella and Dalton, 1990.) Most counselling approaches emphasize the importance of understanding the clients' views of themselves and their problems, but PCP goes furthest, perhaps, in its exploration of how people experience their worlds, how they make sense of themselves and others and the very personal meaning to them of the difficulties they present. Although counsellors have their professional understanding of the anxieties and obstacles which beset those who seek their help, it is the clients' perceptions of the source of those anxieties or the enormity of the obstacles with which we have to work. Our first priority, therefore, is to help them to clarify what is troubling them in the context of their experience of life as a whole.

Developing a system of construing
In *The Psychology of Personal Constructs* (1955), Kelly puts forward his theory of personality, based on his fundamental belief that the way we are is governed by the ways in which we have come to anticipate events. He describes how we try to make sense of things by a process of comparison and contrast. We 'construe'

one person, say, as like someone familiar to us in being 'kind', while a second is 'harsh' in his manner towards us. One situation we have experienced has been 'enjoyable', another 'uncomfortable' and we may anticipate that a third, new situation will be like the second because we have been told that it too will be crowded, noisy and hot. Such bipolar discriminations Kelly refers to as constructs. It should be stressed that constructs are not simply verbalized thoughts – we construe through visual perception (light versus dark), hearing (strident versus mellow), touch (soft versus hard) and smell (sweet versus acrid). And our behaviour itself is seen as an aspect of construing in that by 'behaving' we seek to test out our expectations of the outcome of an action. Many of our constructs are at a low level of awareness. Some past experiences may evoke a gut reaction of fear versus attraction, for example, when we meet someone for the first time.

Kelly sees such constructions as linked together to form networks, as where the person we construe as 'kind' rather than 'harsh' may also seem 'warm' rather than 'cold', 'humorous', rather than 'dour' and so on. Some constructs will be at a higher level of meaning than others. 'Fulfilled' versus 'unfulfilled', for instance, clearly has a wealth of possible meaning, while 'has warm clothes' versus 'has no clothes' may be seen as just one aspect of fulfilment and is therefore said to be subordinate to 'fulfilled/ unfulfilled' which is superordinate to it. Some constructs may be of great significance to the person while others are less important. The former are described as core constructs and the latter as peripheral constructs.

All these constructs, whether easily verbalized or experienced as feelings, abstract or more concrete, core or peripheral are linked together to form a 'construct system'. And it is through this system that a person develops theories about things in order to know how to approach the world. Experience of events and people will modify these theories and elaborate them as we grow older. Our sense of ourselves will change as we become involved in more aspects of life. Learning something new will initiate new ideas. New relationships will evoke new feelings. Validation or invalidation from others will contribute to the overall picture of ourselves at any point in time.

Construing processes

In seeking to understand how people construe things the PCP counsellor goes beyond 'learning the language'. We need to be sure that we have grasped the clients' personal meaning of the words they use and not simply assume it is the same as ours. We also need to learn to read the non-verbal language of posture, gesture and facial expression which will help us to get in touch with feelings which may be difficult to put into words. But taking on the clients' ways of seeing things and trying to put ourselves into their shoes is a process which is concerned not only with the *content* of their construing, but also with the *ways* in which events are approached and experienced.

Kelly's notion of the '*tight versus loose*' dimension in personal construing is a useful one and has important implications for how the counsellor may work with the client. A 'tight' construer is one whose view of life is highly organized, even rigid. He or she will predict from experience that a certain type of person will act in a certain manner and it will be hard to imagine otherwise. There will be difficulty in trying out anything new. A 'loose' construer, on the other hand, may not only change his or her predictions of others very easily but also be a highly unpredictable person. Here the problem may be in following through a line of thought or course of action. Mostly we move from tight to loose in our construing and perhaps only tighten or loosen excessively under threat. But it is important for the counsellor to understand these processes in clients and to help them to modify their approach where it is getting in the way.

A feature of personal construing which also has implications for the counselling process has more to do with *levels* of construing. Some people construe things more meaningfully in quite concrete ways, describing their fellows, for example, in behavioural and physical terms, because that is how personalities come across to them most directly. Others are more inclined to view those about them in relation to more abstract notions such as 'integrity' or 'commitment'. It is important for the counsellor, initially, to tune into the level at which the client is most comfortable. But it may also be necessary, in the interests of movement, to help someone to use other levels of construing – to discover the implications of a physical attribute, for example, in the client's experience of people. Or to encourage those who habitually view things from a philo-sophical height to apply their abstractions to day-to-day events and interactions between people. (The techniques of laddering and pyramiding, described below, are useful here.) This may be particularly relevant in work with those who have communication difficulties. The effects of these problems on relationships has been discussed in Chapter 1. And being stuck in a mode of construing that is either too concrete or too abstract for a fuller under-standing of others may be an important factor (Dalton, 1987, expands on this topic).

Another aspect of the theory which has been found valuable in counselling is Kelly's strong emphasis on the awareness of states of transition. When clients present with a sense of 'not coping' with life it is helpful to look at such feelings in relation to how they experience themselves at the time. Kelly defines the generally vague states of anxiety, guilt and threat in specific terms which can clarify the individual's situation.

Anxiety is seen as an awareness that we are confronted by something of which we have difficulty making sense. We cannot predict other people's behaviour and perhaps not even our own. With a problem like stuttering, which for many people is inter-mittent, not knowing whether they will be able to get through a telephone call or utter the name of the station they want at a ticket office, or whether, when they have to speak at a meeting, words will fail them, can cause chronic uncertainty. Nor can they be sure of other's reactions if they do stutter. One emphasis in counselling with such people would be the alleviation of anxiety through making situations more predictable: if, for example, they are willing to be open about the difficulty and tell people they might have trouble, they can usually anticipate an accepting reaction.

Guilt is seen in terms of dislodgement from core construing of the self – feeling that we are being or doing something out of character. Together client and counsellor may look at what is going on in order to discover whether this feeling is an inevitable result of a sudden change of role or the client is involved in actions which go against some very important aspects of his or her sense of self. Loss of voice is a shock to most people. We take it for granted that we can share in day-to-day exchanges, express our opinions and feelings spontaneously, even earn our living largely by talking. When voice is taken from us we feel cut off, alienated and very much reduced in our ability to take part in many aspects of life.

Threat is the awareness of imminent comprehensive change in the construing of self. Awareness of the implications of change, as with redundancy, loss of a partner or child, even a change of circumstances which will, in theory, be for the better, as with a new job or new relationship, can bring painful feelings and lead to that sense of 'not coping' which is so often expressed. People with long-term communication problems, such as stuttering, mutational voice difficulties or some marked articulatory deviation may work hard to improve, but begin to backtrack when their goals are in sight because the extent of the change in self-perception is too great for them. Too much that is new will be expected of them.

Kelly adds to this list of redefined constructs of transition two more very important aspects of how people can be. With *hostility* he describes the process of a person's clinging to an old stance towards something which has, in fact, proved ineffective. Despite evidence to the contrary, we go on expecting people to behave in certain ways or events to turn out as we always say they will. In the counselling situation, the client may try out something new but 'cook the books' so that the outcome cannot change things. This is generally regarded simply as 'resistance', but the notion of hostility relates such behaviour to the client's fear of having to reconstrue the self if other people are shown to be different or if the client is not as he or she has claimed to be. Another aspect of hostility comes with the denial of loss, say, when a person who has suffered brain damage is unable, together with his or her relatives, for the time at least, to accept that communication will never be as it was.

Aggression, regarded by many as a somewhat doubtful attribute, is redefined as an active readiness to confront new things, to try new ways of dealing with life. Aggressive clients may need little encouragement to explore their situation and to experiment. They will test out fluency or a newly-developed voice in a highly testing situation, perhaps before they are ready for it. In fact, the counsellor's task may be to help clients to consider more carefully the possible outcome of any move they propose to make. They may, typically, be too much inclined to jump in with both feet.

Exploring the client's construing

Kelly himself and others working within a PCP framework have developed a range of procedures for exploring the ways in which clients see themselves and their worlds – that is, for 'subsuming' their construct systems. Careful exploration is seen as essential before any action for change is set in motion. Severe communication problems may preclude the use of some procedures and demand imaginative modification in the use of others, as will be shown in later chapters. The best known of these is repertory grid technique, which is described in detail elsewhere (Fransella and Bannister, 1977; Beail, 1985; Fransella and Dalton, 1990). A brief outline will be given here of methods for eliciting constructs and setting up a simple rated grid, which provides a useful focused sample of the client's construing.

Constructs may be elicited simply through conversation. The counsellor listens for recurring themes and preoccupations, attributions made about other people, events or themselves. A partner may be referred to as 'critical' and when asked how he or she would describe someone who was totally different in this respect the client may say 'accepting'. Clients may refer to themselves as 'cautious', the opposite being viewed as 'impetuous', and so on. A more formal way of eliciting constructs is through triads of people, situations or objects. The person is asked to think of some way in which two of them are alike and different from the third. For example, two events may be seen as 'terrifying', entailing as they do the exposure of the client to public scrutiny. The third event, where he or she is with just one other person, may be contrasted as 'pleasurable'.

We already have some understanding of the words clients are using from the contrasts they make and the contexts within which they make them. A procedure for exploring such constructs further is called 'laddering' (Hinkle, 1965). Here the counsellor asks questions about the construct in order to find out why the client finds a particular contrast meaningful. Here is an example from a client who was concerned with the issue of being 'able to say what you want to say' as opposed to 'finding it hard to express yourself':

Counsellor: You say that some people are able to say what they want to say, while others find it hard to express themselves. Which sort of person would you prefer to be?
Client: The first, of course.
Counsellor: Why?
Client: Well, then people know where they are with you.
Counsellor: Whereas, if you find it hard to express yourself . . .
Client: People are puzzled and may misunderstand you.
Counsellor: Why is it important to you that people should know where they are with you?
Client: They'll trust you then.
Counsellor: But if they're puzzled and perhaps misunderstand you . . .?
Client: They won't know whether they can rely on you.
Counsellor: Why is it important to you to be trusted, relied on?
Client: You don't get anywhere in your job or with friends if you're not.

This is just a small sample of the implications for this particular client of being able to say what you want to say. It involves trust and reliability, essential for both work and social life. For another person the related meanings could be very different – to do with being able to express opinions, perhaps, or coming across to others as intelligent.

Where laddering explores the more abstract meaning of a construct by asking *why* an attribute is important, a technique called pyramiding can clarify *what* a person is getting at by asking for more concrete examples of what he or she is saying. This same client was also concerned with the differences between those who were 'confident' and others who were 'unsure of themselves':

> *Counsellor:* How would you know that someone was confident?
> *Client:* They'd behave quite differently in a situation from me.
> *Counsellor:* What would they do then?
> *Client:* Well, for one thing, they'd walk into a room and feel comfortable.
> *Counsellor:* How would they show that?
> *Client:* They'd be able to go up to people and talk to them, instead of hiding in a corner.
> *Counsellor:* What sort of things would they be able to talk about that you feel you couldn't?
> *Client:* Oh, anything. The weather. The political situation. They could make jokes!

This particular young man, who had had severe articulation problems as a child, found social interaction especially fraught with anxiety, even though his speech was by now intelligible.

By eliciting and exploring a person's construing of things in these and other ways it is possible to obtain a sample of constructs to include in a grid. This allows us to see more clearly the relationships between their important themes, how networks of constructs hang together and where there may be difficulties in achieving some desired change. In Chapter 8 (page 108), an example of a client's grid is shown and discussed.

In *self-characterizations*, also devised by Kelly, clients are asked to write about themselves in the third person, as if through the eyes of an intimate and sympathetic friend. Such a sketch provides client and counsellor with less structured but equally valuable material, showing how the client views him- or herself and what the important themes and preoccupations are. In Chapter 7 (page 84), an example is given and its usefulness examined.

The point should be made here that these and other procedures designed to explore issues with the client will often themselves begin a change process. For example, one client who was laddering 'confident' versus 'not confident', when finding implications of arrogance and insensitivity emerging on the confident pole, which he had said he preferred, changed his mind! Writing a self-characterization can clarify areas of resource which the client has forgotten he or she possessed. And the process of setting up and rating a grid may set in train some ideas for change before any 'analysis' has been made.

The counselling relationship

Few approaches to counselling fail to spell out the importance of empathy with the client, respect for people and their difficulties and the irrelevance of the counsellor's own needs in this situation. These are all included in a PCP discussion of the client–counsellor relationship. Highlighted, too, is the need for the counsellor to be self-reflexive – to be aware of his or her own processes and to recognize that the client will be making something of the counsellor's construing too. In addition, the notion of the counselling process as a 'scientific' activity can provide a useful metaphor. The two people involved are seen as scientists, each contributing, in partnership, to experiments for change. Each has his or her particular expertise. The client has all the 'data', the material from which some resolutions of difficulty may be made. The counsellor has experience in exploring such material and helping the client to make something new out of it.

Applications of a PCP approach to communication problems

The range of communication problems found in children and adults has been outlined in Chapter 1. Although it is possible to some extent to generalize on the various difficulties which can occur for all those, say, with loss of language, dysfluency or voice disorder, the importance of the individuals' experience of them in their own particular contexts cannot be overemphasized. Were this not so, programmed learning or relearning would be the most obvious approach to take. Machines could supplant people in intervention procedures and there would certainly be no need for a counselling component in attempts to alleviate matters.

By now, it should be clear that any disorder of language, voice, articulation or fluency can seriously impede development in the young and cause severe anxiety and loss of self-esteem in older people. With its strong focus on individual experience and core construing or the sense of self, PCP provides a particularly appropriate framework for counselling, where changes in behaviour may depend for their maintenance on changes in self-perception. Equally, where unanticipated change renders a person unable to communicate as before, attention to the experience of guilt, threat and anxiety as described earlier, would seem to be essential alongside attempts to restore or replace communication processes themselves. The exploratory procedures suggested by Kelly and developed by others not only allow us to form a picture of the person we are working with and to understand what the

difficulty means to that person, but they also enable us to anticipate together with that person the implications of any attempts
which may be made to change.

The introduction of PCP into speech and language therapy

In Dunnett's book *Working with People* (1988), I outlined the
development of PCP in what was then called speech therapy. I
attempted to show how this approach, for a growing number of
therapists, has transformed their role from teacher/technician to
one where the counselling aspect of their work has become
paramount. From a narrower focus on 'the problem' there has
been a shift to focusing on 'the person' or persons involved and
the effects that communication difficulties may have on experience
of life as a whole. This has entailed considerable challenge to
earlier approaches and some imaginative adaptations of the work
of practitioners from other disciplines.

With an account of her research project into stuttering Fay
Fransella (1972) first introduced Kelly's ideas into the area of
communication problems. She set out to test the hypothesis that
stuttering would decrease as the meaningfulness of being a fluent
speaker increased. Thus, her emphasis was on the person's 'role' as
a stutterer and change was anticipated through the elaboration of
a new role as a fluent speaker. The work Fransella did with the
people involved in her project was not intended to be 'counselling'
in a full sense, focused as it had to be on the issue of fluency. Yet
the chapter describing personal change in 'Luke', with excerpts
from a taped transcript of sessions, provides excellent examples of
some of the processes involved in PCP counselling in practice. And
the book undoubtedly drew the attention of speech and language
therapists, as well as many others interested in stuttering, to a new
way of approaching dysfluency.

It is not surprising that stuttering is the area which has aroused
the greatest interest in developing a PCP approach to counselling.
The impact of Fransella's work was powerful. And we saw from
the review of the literature in Chapter 1 that, historically,
stuttering has been considered by many as having at least a strong
psychological component, if not to be 'psychogenic' in origin.
Many of us working with dysfluency in the 1970s were dissatisfied
with purely behaviour modification approaches and looking for
something which took into account the complexities of the
experience of stuttering and, above all, the uniqueness of that
experience for particular people. The last twenty years have seen
developments in a PCP approach to stuttering in children
(Hayhow, 1987; Dalton, 1989), in work with individual adults

(Dalton 1987), and with groups (Evesham, 1987). Hayhow and Levy's book, *Working with Stuttering* (1989), presents a comprehensive and integrated framework for working with all ages, with families and with groups. Notably, it also focuses strongly on reflexivity, processes within the therapist/counsellor, which, as was said, is one of the hallmarks of a Kellyan approach.

Chapter 7 is concerned with counselling people with dysfluency problems.

Developments in work with children

In more recent years there has been a growing interest in working with children with communication problems within a PCP framework, largely due to the work of Ravenette. As an educational psychologist he has developed a body of theory and practical techniques designed to help us understand how children make sense of themselves and their situations. We can also see how these views conflict with those of the adults around them. And such understanding may enable child and adult to find alternative ways of dealing with the issues between them.

For children with adequate speech and language, Ravenette's 'structured conversations' (1980) and carefully sequenced questioning (1989) can get us to the heart of what we need to understand. For those who have difficulty in expressing their ideas and feelings, his work with drawing is invaluable. In 'A drawing and its opposite' (1990), for example, he shows how a child may get in touch with very important personal themes, simply through being asked to create one drawing from a given line on a piece of paper and then produce its contrast. Adapting this technique with a child who had withdrawn into silence, a colleague of mine was recently shown just how separate the child felt from her depressed mother and more demanding siblings and how, in the second picture, she imagined what closeness and warmth would be like.

Ideas for the modification of grid techniques for children have been developed by Salmon (1976), Butler (1985) and others. Jackson and Bannister's work on young people's self-characterizations (Jackson and Bannister, 1985; Jackson, 1988) has encouraged the use of writing as part of exploration. And where the extent of the communication problem has precluded the use of either, ideas for careful observation of a child's behaviour from the point of view of its *meaning to the child* have proved enlightening (e.g. Davis and Cunningham, 1985). Asking the Kellyan question 'what behavioural experiment is taking place here?' can be far more fruitful than trying to make sense of what a child is doing in adult terms.

Chapter 10 develops ideas for counselling with children.

Personal reconstruction following brain damage
Brumfitt was probably first to take a PCP approach to those suffering from dysphasia and other speech and language difficulties caused by brain damage. Her findings (1984), which emphasize the extent of the anxiety experienced and the deep sense of loss of self, have influenced many practitioners working in the field to pay more attention to the psychological trauma involved. (More detailed reference will be made in Chapter 9 to Brumfitt's work.)

The development of PCP counselling in the area of neurogenic speech and language difficulties has been held back by the overemphasis on repertory grid technique and other highly verbal procedures associated with Kelly's approach. However, it has proved possible to modify methods for use with children and to invent ways of helping young people to communicate without using sophisticated language. Equally, with some understanding of the implications of different kinds of dysphasia and the perceptual problems which may accompany them, it is possible to adapt existing techniques and to create new ones in order to facilitate communication between client and counsellor (Dalton, 1991). The use of supplied photographic constructs, drawing and music will be described in Chapter 9.

Counselling the relatives of people who have had strokes or suffered brain injury has long been considered an important part of rehabilitation. Much of the work on restoring language may take place at home and it is therefore essential that those involved are helped to understand language processes and language breakdown. However, it is also recognized that spouses, children, other relatives and friends may all suffer some degree of trauma with these events and time and attention has usually been given to what they are experiencing. A PCP approach would seek to understand the ways in which a wife or son, for example, has been dislodged from a familiar role in relation to the dysphasic person. We would listen for any threat to their own core construing and for the effects on the family's dependency system. The extent of anxiety and the degree of threat experienced with change in an important figure in the family constellation needs to be understood. The effects of dysphasia on the relationship between one couple will be described in Chapter 9.

The beginnings of PCP work in other areas
Although the literature shows an increase in the use of counselling in the area of voice disorder, so far there is nothing describing a PCP approach. Yet, in practice, many speech and language therapists who specialize in vocal rehabilitation are finding Kelly's

ideas particularly relevant. Where someone has to have a laryngectomy due to cancer, the experience of total loss of voice has been found to involve a similar impact on the sense of self as someone who has suffered a stroke. Here too there may be loss of role within the family and the workplace. Experiments with various forms of pseudovoice may be impeded by deep anxiety or feelings of alienation, which must be understood by those helping the client.

So-called 'functional' voice disorders, where no organic cause is found, are seen as being partially caused by psychological factors and attention has always been paid to the stresses which underlie them. A PCP approach, however, would look not only at the core constructs involved in the experience of recurrent voice loss or huskiness, but would also seek to anticipate the implications of change if the voice were restored. There may be important meaning in retreating into silence for someone whose situation becomes intolerable. Discovering and sharing that meaning may be a vital step towards finding alternative ways of construing that situation and making it more manageable.

With mutational voice disorders in young males it has been found that elaborating their picture of themselves with appropriate voice quality has been important, alongside any work on lowering pitch and modifying placement. Self-characterizations are useful here, with the opportunity to anticipate the changes that would come about in their lives as a whole. Such writing may emphasize the gains but also reveal some fears that such a radical change in self-perception and the reactions of others might bring. Role play can be helpful for trying out new developments; and the Kellyan use of reverse role play, where the counsellor enacts the client and the client, perhaps, someone with whom he or she has difficulty, can help each of the participants to view both 'characters' in a new light.

Summary

In this chapter an outline has been given of a personal construct approach to communication problems. The pioneering work of Fay Fransella in the area of stuttering, Tom Ravenette's influence on working with children and Sheila Brumfitt's introduction of Kellyan ideas into counselling people with neurological speech and language disorders have been touched on. Work is also being carried out using PCP in relation to voice disorders, although, as yet, this has not been published.

Chapter 3 addresses some crucial issues involved in counselling people with communication problems. These include client expectations, where a 'physical' difficulty may lead to a demand for a physical or 'medical' cure. The practioner may need to find a careful balance between behaviour modification procedures and attention to changes in perception. Behaviour change itself may involve a sense of exposure of the difficulty. In addition, speech and language 'defects' may be regarded as sources of shame and guilt.

3

Crucial Issues in Counselling People with Communication Problems

In Chapter 1 we saw that the term 'counselling' has a wide range of meaning in the literature, ranging from advising the client on the best means of implementing a treatment programme, to dealing with stress factors in the person's environment, to exploring the psychological aspects of a problem as a prime focus of concern. Here, crucial issues will be considered in relation to the processes defined as listening for the clients' meanings and deeper feelings, of helping them to clarify the nature of their problems with themselves and in relationships with others and of discovering their own resources for approaching life more effectively. It is not suggested that all those with communication problems will need such a degree of psychological intervention. However, the focus in this and the following chapters will be on those who could benefit from a counselling approach to their difficulties.

Channels of communication in counselling

The most obvious issue in attempting to bring a counselling dimension to work with those who have impaired communication lies in the very nature of some of the problems themselves. Where a client has a voice or fluency disorder counselling may be largely conversational, although, in severe instances, writing may play a greater part in the exchanges than is usual. However, where language is affected and, particularly, where verbal comprehension is delayed in development or diminished through illness, other means of communication will be needed. Many counsellors use drawing and painting, materials which may be handled, and music and movement, with clients who are verbally able. With those who cannot use language effectively such other media for communication are essential.

'Ben' was 7 years old, but could only speak a few intelligible words. Comprehension was more extensive and his eagerness to communicate and ability to make sense of non-verbal cues meant that he was able to follow clearly-demonstrated instructions. The relationships in his family were troubled and complex and I was concerned to understand how he saw them and his place within them. We played with some pottery models of an assortment of people and established a consistent naming of his mother, father, brother, grandmother and himself. A game was developed placing the different family members together involved in various activities. Then I asked him to show me, with his father's help, who were together at different times of the day: in the morning, after school, at the table in the evening and watching television.

He showed that his father helped him get ready in the morning, while his mother was with his brother. He played (and fought) with his brother after school, sat at a small table with his grandmother for supper and his father helped him to bath before bed while his brother watched television with mother and grandmother. At no point was he engaged in any activity with his mother, whom his crude drawings suggested he adored. This led to a change of direction in conversation with his parents and an exploration of his mother's feelings about having a handicapped child.

'Margaret' had had a stroke, which left her expressive speech severely impaired, although comprehension was much less affected. She was reluctant to draw, although seemed willing for me to get to know her, so that the work we did together should be of real interest to her. Through her responses to a series of pictures of different kinds of people, houses, clothes, food, areas of the country and so on, and to colours, materials and music, I was able to form a profile of her likes and dislikes and, thus, a rough idea of the sort of person she was. When I tentatively fed back to her what my impressions were, she was both pleased and amused. She also wanted to know what my choices were. In that session we established a 'dialogue' which proved an invaluable basis for the future. It led her spontaneously to bring along photographs of people and places that were important to her and she was able to convey something of her feelings about them.

These are just two examples of how non-verbal material may be used to explore aspects of a client's views of things and others will be given in later chapters. Such activity may encourage some clients to use non-verbal communication more freely with others in their environment. And it has been found that taking the emphasis off the *struggle* to speak can in itself facilitate spontaneous verbal expression. Even where verbal communication is not severely impaired, attempting to express something through drawing, modelling, or the sounds of a musical instrument may help the person to get in touch with feelings that can be masked by words. The counsellor needs to be inventive and to encourage experimentation in clients, who may find that they have resources within themselves that have never before been tapped.

Learning to converse
Less obvious than the lack of verbal or vocal skills in many of these clients is the failure to learn to listen and to respond appropriately in conversational interchange. Anxiety about their own 'performance', for example, preoccupies many people who stutter, to the extent that they are unable to take in a conversation around them. Fearful that they will be asked a question which will be difficult to answer, it does not occur to them to focus on others, ask something of them, or show an interest in something outside themselves. If language has been a struggle while growing up, they may not have been asked their opinions or how they felt about things. Not only is 'the art of conversation' beyond them, but also the process of expressing their thoughts and feelings in words is something new to be learned.

The counsellor may find that it takes some time for such clients to go beyond one-word answers to questions put to them or to elaborate on what a particular experience has meant to them. One young man was sent to see a psychotherapist because of his failure to relate to his peers in his senior school. Although he had progressed academically after a slow linguistic development, he was silent, isolated and sometimes quite aggressive in his social awkwardness. The therapist believed in leaving the client to set the agenda and, after greeting him, waited. For two sessions they sat without exchanging a word. The boy was able to explain later that he simply did not know what was expected of him and could think of nothing to say. The counsellor with whom he then worked took his lack of experience into account and, to begin with, contributed more to their exchanges until he had learned to express things more readily.

Clients' expectations

Most clients, if you ask them, have theories about their problems. A young dysfluent child may believe that words become 'stuck' in the throat. One such little boy said that he tried to cough to get the words out. A teacher with recurrent voice loss put it all down to the emissions from her neighbour's boiler, despite the fact that she was unhappy in her work and the dysphonia recurred at the beginning of each school term. She was unwilling to believe that stress played any part in her difficulty, as that would imply that she was 'not coping'. Someone who has had a stroke and is receiving physiotherapy to help restore physical movement may see language drills as equivalently appropriate for the rehabilitation of speech. The notion that attention to feelings of loss and anxiety might help the process of coming to terms with change could be quite alien. Guilt in relation to a life-style which is seen to have contributed to a condition such as cancer of the larynx has been known to dishearten a person from attempting to communicate again.

Some clients will give expression to their theories quite freely and are willing to explore current views of their situation. One young man who stuttered severely had been convinced for years that it was a punishment for mocking a dysfluent school-fellow. While accepting the seriousness of the guilt which he had carried around with him for so long, it was possible to help him to forgive himself as he had been brought up to forgive others all his life. He too 'deserved' to progress now. Whatever the theory held as to the cause of a problem, however bizarre or negative its implications, it has to be the starting point for counselling and, along with expectations of 'treatment', renegotiated with care if the client is not to feel rejected and confused.

Psychological intrusion

More difficult to approach through counselling is the clients' conviction that what is wrong is physical and only physical. They see the practioner as there to 'cure' the problem – to offer medicine, mechanical repair or exercises. Being asked about their feelings, about their views of themselves and their place in their worlds is experienced as an intrusion and this must be respected. Psychological intervention can never be imposed on people. Counsellors in all areas of difficulty know that someone who is 'sent' for help because others think they need it may see no point in delving into emotions or reflecting on the meaning of events. It is even less likely that a clinician who feels that a client with a communication problem 'needs' counselling where he or she is not interested will do more than irritate and possibly render less effective any practical measures which may be employed.

We also have to recognize that many people, especially older people, are quite antagonistic towards 'psychologists' and have firm beliefs about dealing with life's blows as they come, either on their own or with the support of family and a few close friends. Anyone who attempts to 'put them in touch with their feelings' will be given short shrift. The last thing some people who have suffered a stroke, for example, want to do is to be helped to express their grief in tears. They are there to get on with the business of speaking and walking again. If the counsellor/therapist respects their wishes and is alongside them in their struggle for recovery, a degree of acceptance and understanding of their feelings that is at the heart of any counselling may be experienced.

Working with parents

Working with the parents of communicatively impaired children also requires sensitivity towards expectations of the help that is on offer, together with awareness of the guilt and anger that may underlie their approach to the situation. The parents have theories about the causes of the problems. The child with unintelligible speech is 'lazy', dysfluency is 'an attention-seeking device'. The mother may blame herself for her child's difficult birth which is said to have caused the language delay. There may be conflict between the parents as to whose side of the family is responsible for transmitting the stuttering. Any judgemental reflection on the ways in which they bring up their children may be met with hostility or cause loss of confidence in themselves as parents.

This is not simply to imply that the clinician needs to be tactful. It is important to give adequate time to exploring the parents' attitudes and their feelings about any part they may have played in their child's difficulty and what they will be expected to contribute towards its amelioration. Some may feel that having handed over the problem to 'the expert', that is all that will be required of them. Others are anxious to help and willing not only to learn about the management of the problem itself, but also to view what has to be done in the light of the child's needs as a whole. A working relationship with those caring for young people needs to be established for progress to be made and this may involve ongoing attention to the difficulties that they experience within the family or within their wider social group.

Psychological difficulty: cause or effect?

It was implied above that many people prefer to see their problem, or that of a child, as physical in origin and therefore amenable to some tangible, physical 'cure'. Where there is clearly a psychological component, however, with anxiety or depression enmeshed with stuttering or dysphonia, aggressive behaviour or withdrawal in children with inadequate language, there may be confusion as to what kind of help should be sought. Am I depressed and anxious because I cannot rely on my voice to hold out in some activity which is important to me or is it the stress around that activity which is too much for me? Is my child angry and frustrated because he cannot communicate or is there some other trauma blocking him?

With stuttering, as has been said already, there may be sharply opposing views among clinicians and clients as to the appropriate form of treatment. If the dysfluency is believed to have been caused by a traumatic experience in childhood or an ongoing neurosis, the person may turn to psychotherapy or hypnosis. Unfortunately, though, these approaches alone do not seem to be effective in unravelling the complex behavioural patterns that can develop over time and become themselves a focus of negative self-perception. Equally, expectations that a structured speech modification programme of itself will lead to lasting fluency have been disappointed, where the person's anticipations of speech failure have not also been changed.

Where there is an acquired speech or language problem in later life, the longer-term psychological effects will clearly relate to that person's sense of him- or herself before the illness. A person may become deeply depressed by the onset of dysphasia. If he or she has not experienced depression before, then work to restore language will contribute to recovery. It may be, however, that someone who has been depressed for much of his or her life will not have the motivation for language work and attention needs to be focused on helping that person to make sense of this latest catastrophe.

Finding a balance

In many cases, it is not a question of whether psychological *or* practical treatment should be offered, but of finding an appropriate balance between the two. This will depend on a number of factors, namely, the severity of the communication problem itself, the degree to which the person is affected psychologically by the difficulty and, above all, the client's wishes. The severity of the problem will not necessarily be measurable externally. Clearly, where a young child is unable to speak or comprehend language, or a person has had no voice for a period of time, it is an objectively serious matter. But we cannot assume that someone who rarely stutters overtly, for example, does not feel handicapped by a fear of dysfluency or that someone with slightly deviant articulation is not painfully self-conscious, especially if teased about it.

The clients' perception of their problems will affect their ability to respond to direct speech, language or voice work. Someone who is overwhelmed by anxiety may well find it impossible early on to carry out experiments for change. A stutterer who is avoiding situations through fear of speech failure will not readily go into them using a behavioural technique. A young person with a mutational voice disorder may be too embarrassed to attempt to use a lower register anywhere other than in the clinic. In these and other instances much work may be needed to help the clients overcome their lack of confidence and sense of social failure, before they are ready to test out new ways of communicating.

The parents of young children and those caring for people with acquired speech disorders may need extensive counselling before they can contribute to their family member's difficulty. Where parental anxiety or hostility, or a spouse's anger or despair are forming a barrier to progress, time will be well spent in building a relationship of trust and cooperation. The relatives may be demanding 'results', but forging ahead with a programme of structured work could prove fruitless, unless the implications of what is being attempted are made clear and the likely outcome prepared for.

The role of the counsellor/clinician

Anyone working in this area, where the client needs both direct work and psychological help, will need to find a way of combining the very different skills required. As Miller (1990a: 2) points out, at one level the speech and language therapist may be listening and 'analysing language for its content, form or use'. As a counsellor he or she will 'listen for the feelings behind what a person is trying to say' and the very individual meaning of the words spoken. It is often necessary to advise quite directly on the ways in which new means of communicating may be carried out or exercises performed. As far as the person's psychological difficulties are concerned, 'advice' is not given. Unless clinicians are clear in their own minds as to which mode they are in, both they and the clients may become confused.

One way of avoiding confusion is for direct work to be undertaken by one professional and counselling by another, as described in Chapter 1, where clinical psychologists and speech and language therapists work together on stuttering and voice problems. This can prove effective if the two are in close communication, with the client's consent. Alternatively, the sessions may be clearly divided between the two kinds of work. For example, if someone is learning a fluency technique, part of the session may be devoted to this and the rest to issues of personal difficulty. In the early stages, it will not be possible for the client to maintain speech modification throughout and the counsellor should not attempt to encourage the client to try. A third approach is for direct work to be undertaken in groups and for counselling to take place on an individual basis. I have found it useful to do the psychological groundwork with people who stutter before they go on a speech course, and/or to help them afterwards with problems of maintaining change and making further changes in self-perception.

Communication 'defects' as matters of shame and guilt

One of the issues common to the whole range of communication problems is the degree of shame or guilt which may be experienced by clients and their families. Any handicap might be regarded as a 'flaw', rather than a difficulty to be overcome. Ben's mother, referred to earlier, was deeply distressed by her son's inadequacies, ashamed of his behaviour in public and filled with guilt at having produced a child who was not 'normal'. Many parents are less overtly rejecting, but still angry at having to cope and they sometimes project this anger onto the professionals who are perceived as not doing enough to help. The spouse of someone who has had a stroke may be both hurt and embarrassed by his or her failures in communication. These feelings need to be understood.

In the clients themselves, shame may develop very early. Many adults have memories of feeling deeply invalidated at school and at home and carry these feelings with them as they grow older. Even with success in overcoming dysfluency, developing normal voice or recovering language skills, the person's sense of self may remain fragile. This is why, in this area of counselling in particular, it seems important for the door to be left open, for the client to feel able to return for further help when old anxieties and self-doubts are stirred up by events. However, this is not to encourage undue dependency – clients alone can rediscover their resources to help themselves. In my experience, however, there is so much for them to come to terms with that many clients can only deal with the necessary changes in 'layers'.

The threat of change

Much has been written about 'resistance' to therapy or counselling. This may take a number of forms from over-intellectualization, with a failure to access let alone express feelings, to 'learned helplessness', where the client waits passively for nothing to happen. A client in any area of counselling may have great difficulty in risking change, but for those with communication problems the risks may be even greater. They too may have to give up long-held beliefs about themselves as being hopeless and incapable of taking responsibility. They also may be called upon to question their views of other people and of the meaning of past events. But there are other ways in which their sense of themselves may be challenged. Our voice, our speech patterns, our use of language are very much expressions of our personalities. To change any of them, however poorly we regard them, can be to become unrecognizable to oneself.

I have already referred to the difficulties young men with mutational voice disorders may have in using a lower pitch of voice in public. These young men may hate the recorded sound of their undeveloped voice, but it is the sound they know inside their heads and the new voice is not only alien to themselves but unfamiliar to others and may draw unwelcome comments. Burk and Brenner (1991) stress the need to listen first to the feelings of voice-disordered young people concerning voice difference, before launching into an 'action-orientated' programme of work with them. The huskiness or hoarseness, again, may have become part of their self-image and although it is important to help them not to damage their voices further, the change needs to be gradual enough for them to come to terms with it.

Those who have had a laryngectomy have an even greater change to face if they learn to produce sound from the oesophagus (a kind of modified burp) or use any kind of mechanical voice. Excellent as many oesophageal speakers are, there may be great reluctance, especially in women, to adopt the distinctively different sound for purposes of day-to-day communication. Artificial voices have improved considerably over the last few years and many are willing to use them, rather than remain silent. But it takes courage to join in conversations with others, particularly in social situations.

For people with neurologically acquired speech and language problems, it may be difficult to learn to use new channels of communication, such as gesture, communication boards and mechanical devices. It may be very painful to acknowledge that these things are needed, particularly where someone has been highly articulate. Many such people show remarkable resilience in the face of deeply frustrating experience. But for some, one of the counsellor/clinician's main tasks may be to clarify the implications of the choices they have to make between cutting themselves off from the world or managing whatever means are available to facilitate interaction with others.

Stuttering is perhaps the problem which is most resistant to change. Not only is it difficult to maintain a learned fluency in the face of pressure and anxiety, but the many other behaviours and self-perceptions which have developed around the dysfluency make the transition from stutterer to fluent speaker a very complex one. Added to this, where the person has chosen to keep quiet, to avoid or substitute many words, to stay away from situations which will reveal the difficulty, the fear of exposure may, for a time at least, prevent their making any progress outside the clinical setting. As we shall see in Chapter 7, awareness on the part of the counsellor of what may for a particular individual be an almost intolerable threat is essential.

Producing 'results'

The clients' and relatives' expectations when they seek help for a communication problem have been discussed above. Many, understandably, anticipate a 'cure'. They may have traipsed from one professional to another, responded to advertised claims, put all their resources towards paying for a new method of treatment for stuttering, language impairment, articulation defect or chronic voice loss, all in vain. Someone offering counselling as an aspect of an approach to their difficulties may be seen simply as preparing those concerned for partial success or help with 'learning to live with it'. The counsellor/clinician may indeed, after exploring the client's condition, feel that he or she is unlikely to progress as far as is hoped. A severely brain-damaged child or adult will be limited in capacity to learn or re-learn. Someone who has stuttered severely for many years may well be seen as unable to make the enormous and complex changes necessary for sustained fluency. It may be impossible for a person whose voice expresses the stress in his or her life to make a change in that lifestyle.

If, during the exploratory phase, trust and mutual respect are established between counsellor and client or the client's family, it should be possible for expectations to be revised and energies channelled into what *can* be done. The clinician's understanding of the situation will then be seen not as the counsel of despair but of hope. In time there may be great relief that the long chase after a miracle is over and hence real acceptance of the client as he or she is, leaving more scope for genuine development. I have seen this occur with the parents of a dysphasic child and with a number of severely dysfluent people.

In one instance, however, a young man whose dysfluency was neurological in origin was beginning to speak more socially and to make friends for the first time in his life. His parents, although disappointed that the work we were doing had not made him more fluent, acknowledged that he was happier and more confident. Then his grandparents came to visit and were furious at the change in him. They had been used to his remaining silent and biddable most of the time and were shocked that he joined in conversations and made them wait while he expressed his opinions. They insisted that he was deteriorating and demanded that treatment should stop at once. The parents were very uncertain as to what to do, but the young man was determined to carry on. The 'results' were undoubtedly more beneficial to him than a number of behavioural treatments he had undergone without success. But, from the outside, the aspect of the problem which troubled others was not being addressed. And this may be the case with many clients. Therapists working with people with severe dysphasia have always found it difficult to quantify progress for external audit. If a client is able to speak little more after a series of sessions combining counselling with direct work, but is no longer depressed, how is this to be measured and presented to those 'buying in' the clinician's services?

One useful way of looking at the outcome of working with communication disorders has been outlined by Enderby (1992). She considers dysphasia in particular in relation to four aspects: impairment, disability, handicap and distress. The impairment suffered by the client lies in such problems as word-finding difficulty or loss of grammatical structure. The disability may be a resultant lack of coherence and failure to interact with others. The handicap is manifested in lack of confidence and the limitations in fulfilling the person's potential. Varying degress of distress will be experienced by both the person and his or her relatives. It is to the third and fourth of these dimensions that a counselling approach to dysphasia may contribute most. Speech and language may or may not improve greatly over time. But the counsellor/clinician's concern is also with the quality of people's lives. In Chapter 9 an example is given of work with a dysphasic person and his wife where counselling is the main resource used.

It could be said that using a counselling approach to any communication problem is addressing first and foremost the handicap and distress experienced by the client. This does not imply that direct work on aspects of a disorder does not in itself aim at reducing the handicap and thus the distress experienced. However, the counsellor's concern with the person as a whole, with the effects on the sense of self, and on relationships with others that these difficulties can bring widens the focus. It can help the client to reach beyond concern with attaining improved communication only. It can lead the client to experience what human communication is *for*, by attempting new activities and coming to understand a range of new people.

Summary

The purpose of this chapter has been to pin-point some of the main issues which may arise when counselling people with difficulties in speech, language or voice. The need for finding non-verbal means of communicating has been stressed and for taking into account a person's lack of experience in expressing thoughts and feelings. The importance of clarifying the clients' theories about their problems and their expectations of what help will involve has been discussed, together with ways in which a balance between direct work and counselling may be found. The threats involved in change have also been outlined. Finally, the part played by counselling in reducing the *handicapping* effect of communicative impairment and the resultant *distress* has been put forward.

In the next chapter, on beginning counselling, the focus will be on setting the scene. Means of exploring the clients' current ways of approaching their problems and their lives as a whole will be suggested. How 'contracts' might be negotiated, according to the clients' needs, whether it be for a combination of direct work and counselling or for counselling only will be discussed. The setting of appropriate initial goals and the estimation of the time that will be needed to achieve them will also be discussed. Throughout, the clients' approach to their communication problems will be considered in relation to their personalities as a whole and in the context of the lives they lead.

4

Beginning Counselling

A counsellor brings to that first meeting with a new client the theoretical framework and practical guidelines of his or her training, together with all that has been learned from working with other clients. Counsellors also bring their own life experience and the understanding of themselves that they have gained through supervision and personal counselling. Although training and life experience will vary from one person to another, certain basic principles of working with people who ask for psychological help will be implicit in their approach.

First, there is a willingness to *listen* to what clients have to say and attempt to understand things from their point of view. Along with this comes *acceptance* of people *as they are* and of the validity of their views of their difficulty. There is also the feeling of *responsibility*, when someone confides in us, to help them as best we can. And this will involve being aware of our *own experience* in the process of counselling as it develops. Which starts with the first contact.

First contacts

Adult clients seeking counselling refer themselves, either by telephone or by letter or may be referred by other professionals, usually in the form of a written recommendation, whether it is within the NHS or Community Service or to a private practitioner. The nature of this initial contact will affect the counsellor's expectations of the first meeting in some way and he or she needs to be fully aware of any impressions that are formed. A telephone contact, for example, may convey a client's anxiety very clearly or an assumed casualness attempt to convey the notion that there is some small problem which it might be useful to talk through. Either approach will be a first indication of how the person wishes to present him- or herself to a stranger.

Being grilled about one's qualifications and training by a prospective client, just as you are about to eat, may be awkward, but clients have a right to question and to 'shop around'. An attempt to beat a private practitioner down with regard to fees before any hint is given as to who they are or why they are calling could simply irritate or, again, be seen as signalling an important preoccupation. Counsellors too will be demonstrating something of their approach by their response. They too are being construed by the client. I was put off some years ago when contacting a therapist by telephone. A few seconds into the conversation she began asking me for intimate details of myself and my life – clearly taking a case history on the spot. I did not follow this up. There is no optimal way of responding at this point. Only a need to be sensitive to what both of you might be experiencing.

Letters from clients often provide more useful material. Sometimes they are long and detailed and a strong impression of the writers' attitudes towards their difficulties is given. We may pick up important themes and predominant feelings, which recur throughout sessions. Even a very brief request for a meeting can tell us something, from the formality or informality of the style, the literacy or otherwise and the writing. A bold, flourishing hand will conjure up a very different picture from one which is small and neat. I am not suggesting that any kind of early 'diagnosis' should be made from these clues, only that counsellors be aware of any expectations that have been roused in them.

Written referrals from other professionals can give the barest information or take the form of a case history, with the referrer's views as to the client's needs clearly spelt out. These I am tempted to leave unread until I have met the person, not wishing to have my own first impressions influenced by them. One psychiatrist referred a man to me, of whom he clearly disapproved, asking me to 'instil in him some moral values'! On the other hand, where counselling forms part of a team approach to a number of difficulties, as in the case of someone who has suffered a head injury, it is important to take the attitudes of others working with the client into account, which may be shown from the tone of the referral. The client may be setting up a negative 'reputation', which, on reflection, he or she would wish to reverse.

Where someone has a communication problem, these initial contacts can give the counsellor confusing messages. Most notably, people who stutter may experience their greatest difficulty on the telephone. Many of them would choose to write, but those who phone may come across as deeply anxious, brusque and aggressive or, if they change words in their effort to remain fluent, almost incoherent. Similarly, people with voice problems often find telephoning stressful and feel particularly 'not themselves' when they have only their voices to present to a stranger. Although it is important to register the impression they make in this context, since it will reflect the impression they give to others, we must be open to something very different when we meet them face to face.

Referring children

It is often pointed out that when children are referred for psychological help it is not usually they who think they have a problem. Someone else is bothered by their behaviour, their response to teaching, or their failure to do something in the way that is expected of them. They do not refer themselves and it is even more important that the counsellor pay attention to the terms in which the young person is referred than with adults. When a parent or a teacher or some other person involved with the child describes what they perceive to be the problem we need, as Ravenette (1987) has pointed out, to discover what impact the behaviour or the failure has on *them*. Is some important belief about their role as parents or teachers or how children 'should' be being challenged? Do they see themselves as responsible for the child's difficulty?

Children with communication problems may or may not be aware that they are causing anxiety. A young dysfluent child is not always conscious of repeating syllables, words or phrases. A child with a language problem can take some time to realize that anything is wrong. Where children are aware, however, their perception of the problem will undoubtedly be very different from that of the adults concerned. What the latter may see as a potential source of social handicap, the former may experience, very much in the moment, as confusing, frustrating or even something that seems to make them 'special'. Like the little boy referred to in the last chapter as feeling the words getting stuck in his throat, the child's experience is likely to be essentially physical and emotional. An older child's priorities, too, will be different from those of parents or teachers. The inability to join in the pursuits of fellows or to make friends may be far more important than future job prospects.

When preparing to work with children, any clues as to the theories and attitudes of concerned adults and the young people themselves need to be weighed equally, where both will be involved in the work you do.

First meetings

Most other areas of counselling will take place in a limited range of settings: a room set aside in an institution (albeit more closely resembling a cupboard in some); a room in the counsellor's house or the client's. We have to add to these, when considering possible contexts for seeing people with communication problems for the first time, a room in a hospital, a busy ward, even an intensive care unit. It will be clear that the possibilities for establishing a relationship or beginning to make an assessment of the person's needs in the hospital situation will be very different.

In the more private settings, some of the essential elements in that first face-to-face meeting will be similar whatever the presenting problem. The counsellor will try to establish what the client's expectations are. In the case of those with communication difficulties, how much are these focused on working directly on the impairment itself and how far does the client see the psychological aspects as an important part of what you will be doing together? Do clients come with a sense of needing to change the ways they are handling the problem or wanting to relate differently to people or feel better about themselves? As with all those we work with, the clients' stories are very important and how they see themselves as becoming who they are. What hopes have they for change? And is this change to come from the clinician alone as 'the expert'? Some of their expectations may be influenced by other experiences of help, whether from another counsellor or some other professional.

A counsellor/practitioner may feel with the client that both direct work and psychological work are needed. And although it will probably be too soon to negotiate exactly what will be attempted, some idea must be given of what each aspect might entail. Someone with a voice problem, for example, may need practical strategies for conserving the voice, relaxation techniques or other exercises. At the same time, it may be felt that the person's general stress level should be explored, that relationships with others are a major source of anxiety and lack of confidence causing feelings of hopelessness. An agreement can be reached on how best to combine both kinds of work, so that the counsellor is able to plan the early sessions and the client knows what to expect.

In some instances, the nature of the impairment itself will call for other than purely verbal channels of communication to be employed. Again, it will not be possible to decide on this aspect during the first session. But it is possible to check on whether the client is comfortable with writing or drawing, for example. Byrne (1987) refers to the use of writing during her early work with those who stutter very severely. A client on 'voice rest' might do better to write, rather than whisper, since a tense, forced whisper can do as much harm to the vocal cords as shouting. Where there are linguistic difficulties, however, writing will probably be as difficult as speaking. If language is not too severely affected, as with mild dysphasia in an adult, it will be for the clinician to assess the particular areas of difficulty, make some adjustment in his or her own verbalization to the client and perhaps to suggest that when speaking of personal things 'accuracy' need not be a priority.

Where language is severely impaired in a child or an adult, it may only be possible during this first session to discover what means of communication are viable. It is important to convey that you are interested in the *person* as well as there to help with language. Someone who has recently had a stroke has probably already been asked the name of the prime minister and the price of a loaf of bread by a junior doctor or two. The patient will be understandably confused, even infuriated, by having objects waved in front of him or her with a demand for names or being asked to put the spoon in the cup or the pen on top of the handkerchief. Essential as a thorough assessment is, at this stage establishing who you are, through simple drawings perhaps, showing that you understand the client's difficulty with speech, with the help of mime, and indicating that you would like to help him or her are more urgent. If the client is in hospital, the first visit may be quite short. If at home, there will be more time to encourage the use of drawing, to use any photographs available, and to enlist the help of a relative to tell you something about the client and his or her needs.

When seeing a child with a severe language problem for the first time a parent is usually present. There may have been an earlier meeting with the mother or both parents. The counsellor will have begun to understand something of the parents' views of the situation and how the child's difficulty affects the family as a whole. It should be possible to establish how the meeting with the child, for example a little girl, can be prepared: would she feel more comfortable if she brought something of her own to play with or to show the counsellor? What does she enjoy doing? Although the child may be used to others talking over and around her, it will be important to negotiate that communication with her and from her, by whatever means, will be the main focus of the session. In this instance, counselling sessions will be arranged for the parents, who have asked for help in managing their daughter's difficulty. Work with the child will first be focused on establishing a trusting relationship and a context within which she can express her feelings and experience acceptance at every level.

Seeing any child with a parent present gives the counsellor an opportunity to observe their interaction. A child may be shy and look to mother for guidance before sitting down or engaging in any activity. The mother may seem anxious about the child's behaviour and tell the child to sit still or not to touch things. In contrast, another child may come into a room with confidence, explore the surroundings, drawing the mother's attention to this or that and quickly engage with a stranger. The parent's reaction to, for example, a child's dysfluency or failure to communicate, will tell us something of a general response, whether it be of irritation, anxiety or relaxed acceptance. Sometimes it becomes clear that the child is something of a little tyrant, with mother attempting to placate all the time. Her apparent lack of confidence, at least in her role as mother, may prove an important focus of sessions with her alone.

Where a child is older and verbal communication more appropriate, the issue of confidentiality arises. It is likely that the counsellor will speak with the parents too and it is necessary to agree with all concerned at the outset what the 'rules' are. The parents can be assured that what they say will not be passed on to the child; the child, likewise, should feel able to speak freely. It should be established, however, that where the counsellor feels it important for something to be shared between family members, in order to improve understanding or change some damaging pattern of interaction, he or she will negotiate with them to do so. As with all clients, only where the child might harm him- or herself, or others if nothing is said or no action taken will confidentiality be broken. (This issue is explored further in Chapter 10.)

During the first session with a child alone, it is important to discover why the child thinks he or she is there, what the counsellor's expectations are imagined to be, and what is most troubling to the child. One 12-year-old with a repaired cleft lip and palate had had a good deal of therapy to improve her speech and was due for further surgery in a few months' time. She was sullen and restless and apparently had difficulty concentrating at school. She 'supposed' that we would practise reading, which she disliked, and seemed surprised when I asked her what she most enjoyed about life and what she most wanted to change about herself. She enjoyed, more than anything, being out walking with her dog. She didn't want to change anything about herself, only to find out what was wrong with the others at school, who didn't like her and didn't want her for a friend. I suggested that rather than practise reading we might spend some time talking about these things which were important to her. The first few sessions focused mainly on looking at what friendship was about.

We must never forget, of course, that while we are attempting to form an impression of our clients and their needs, they are busy trying to make sense of us. Our attitude to them, together with memories of former encounters, will play its part in the picture of us they take away from the first meeting. Once again, there is no 'model' of behaviour for counsellors. But in general we need to be natural and, while showing that we have some understanding of their situation, not assume an air of all-knowing mystery. We need to be welcoming, without being too garrulous. Above all, we need to convey our willingness to focus on them and their concerns and be sensitively aware of the effects of anything which we might say or do.

The initial 'contract'

Some of what has been discussed already forms part of an initial agreement with a client or members of the family: what the focus of the early session will be in terms of direct work and/or counselling, decisions as to who will be involved and to what extent. What many people will ask is 'Can you cure my stutter/my voice problem/my child's unintelligible speech/my wife's loss of language?' And next, 'How long will it take?' Neither question will be possible to answer at this stage. Even if it is made clear that the work to come will depend as much on what they put into it as on what we have to offer, it may be some time before some of those involved are able to accept that we do not have all the answers. If we warn people that a 'cure' may not be possible, they will not always hear us.

What we *can* do is suggest a number of sessions during which certain specific procedures will be undertaken. It may be necessary to assess the nature and degree of the communication problem itself. In addition, the counsellor will need time to explore the psychological aspects with the client, in order to clarify further the balance of the approach that will be taken. Where clients come with an expressed need for counselling uppermost in their minds, there may be no need for formal assessment. An estimate of the time needed to gain a full picture of what is involved will govern the number of sessions negotiated. After which, the situation will be reviewed and a plan for a series of sessions with agreed aims be offered.

Exploring the problem, understanding the person

As this is a book about counselling rather than speech and language therapy, this section will provide some examples of how we might set about exploring the psychological implications of a communication problem and come to an understanding of the client who is experiencing it and/or family members who will be involved in its alleviation. (As has been said, it may also be necessary to undertake a voice, fluency, language or articulation assessment during these early sessions.)

Whatever the presenting problem it is helpful to gain some idea of how people see themselves and their situation and how they relate to the people and events in their world. This may be done through conversation or through writing, such as the self characterization described in Chapter 2. A counsellor using a PCP approach may find setting up a grid an economical way of focusing on major themes (see pp. 19–21). Asking clients to draw 'life-lines', indicating crucial events and marking off distinct phases in their personal history is another way of looking at how they have come to where they are now. Ravenette's 'Who are you?' technique, illustrated in Chapter 10, consists of some carefully structured questions aimed at exploring the meaning of some important attributes which clients apply to themselves and perceive others as applying to them.

These and other procedures are some of the many verbal ways of building a picture of the whole person. Through them clients have the opportunity of expressing their sense of self, which may be clearly defined in negative or positive ways, shadowy or confused. We can also gain an impression of some of the important people in their worlds, of crucial events they see as influencing them and issues which preoccupy them. Just as important, we would hope to gain some idea of the *ways* in which they view things: do they look for black-and-white certainties or are they happy to consider alternatives? Are their perceptions of the world constricted to a narrow range of concerns or do they look more widely beyond themselves? How have they approached significant events in the past? What unnecessary limitations have they set on themselves? What are their resources?

Where the parents of young children feel that counselling sessions would be helpful to them, conversation will be the main medium of exchange, but here, too, writing may be useful. Asked to write a description of their child, mothers in particular will often go beyond expressing their frustrations and anxieties about the effects that the problem has on the child in question. We are given a picture of the family as a whole, with comparisons made with siblings or similarities and differences drawn between the child and the parents themselves. They may reflect on their own earlier or current difficulties and disappointments. All this will contribute to our understanding of what they need not only to help the child but, perhaps, to review their attitudes towards themselves.

Where a client's speech or writing are restricted, the counsellor may gain some insights through drawing or painting. Simply asking for a representation of something which makes the person feel good and, in contrast, something which has the opposite effect can pin-point significant aspects of that person's experience. A young boy who had chosen not to speak first drew a picture of himself alone on a swing, then, in heavy black crayon, showed a group of people, crowded tightly together, their mouths open, fists clenched in the air. I suggested a number of people whom they might be, including his family and people at school and he nodded yes to all of them. A man who was unable to speak due to a stroke drew how he saw himself in relation to his wife and child for a colleague of mine. Crude as the drawing was, done with his non-preferred hand, the sense of closeness to his son and distance from his wife was movingly conveyed. It showed the focus of what concerned him most about his condition.

Where a young child is unable to draw or an adult unwilling or unable, we may only have non-verbal behaviour to go on in our attempts to understand what their experiences mean to them. Watching a child play with figures and objects can give us some tentative ideas, but it is important not to pre-empt an 'interpretation' of an action. Throwing things around *may* mean that the child is angry or destructive, but it may show excitement and a sense of freedom. Observation of facial expresssion and general body movement will suggest which. Davis and Cunningham (1985) give an instance of how putting a particular piece of behaviour in the context of their general impressions of a child led them to suggest its true meaning to her frustrated mother. She had viewed her attempts to touch boiling saucepans as 'getting at me for not taking notice of her'. They had observed similar actions and facial expressions when the mother was cleaning or ironing and wondered whether she was not, in fact, 'trying to help'. When a pretend stove was placed in the kitchen the troublesome behaviour stopped.

An example has been given in Chapter 2 of how a relationship was established with 'Margaret', whose communication was severely limited by dysphasia. Unable to talk about herself and reluctant to draw she was willing to share something of herself through her selection or rejection of pictures of people, houses, colours and so on. With an elderly actor in a similar situation, whom I saw in hospital, photographs from his childhood and of productions in which he had taken part formed the basis for building a 'life-story', which meant a great deal to him and gave me a strong impression of his experiences and of what he had lost. His wife, who initially believed that restoring his ability to speak was the only thing that mattered, gradually contributed more to this aspect of our work. As she eased her pressure on him to speak, rather than use the gesture and mime which came naturally to him, he relaxed and, in fact, was able to verbalize to some extent spontaneously.

Setting the early goals

The exploratory phase of counselling in this area should enable us to accomplish a number of important things: to establish a working relationship with the client and anyone else who may need to be involved; to discover the most effective means of communicating with each other; to learn the extent to which the problem is affecting the person's sense of self or influencing the family system; and, finally, through an understanding of how the people concerned approach life as a whole, to pin-point those areas where change seems to be needed and those where resources may be found to bring about such change. In the last of the preliminary sessions agreed on the counsellor will draw things together and present the client with a suggested plan of action.

Immobilization or change?

During four sessions with a young woman who stuttered she produced a self-characterization, which showed her life to have been dominated by her attempts to hide her dysfluency. We explored the meaning of her experiences as a child at school, where she responded to early teasing by withdrawal behind a barrier of aloofness and hard work, making no friends. We looked at the ways in which her family had reacted, which largely consisted of denial of any real difficulty and led her to hide it even from them. When she described how she related to people at work, the apparent aloofness persisted and she firmly believed that no one knew that she stuttered. If they did they would despise her. She was stuck and realized that she could go no further in her career or in her social life unless she risked exposing her dysfluency.

She saw that she had a choice between remaining trapped in what she called her 'pretence' and testing out her theory about people's reactions if they heard her stutter. It took her a while to admit how much she wanted friendship and it was clear that she knew little about it. She would also need to learn to relate to others, to include them in her scheme of things if her life was to become richer. Most of all she needed to review her beliefs about herself as flawed, misunderstood. We looked at this formidable set of tasks and discussed how she might begin to accomplish them through small experiments in speaking more openly to one or two people, learning to observe and listen to others, in order to come to know them and so on. We agreed to work together weekly for three months to begin with and see how far she could go.

Facing the future

When I began working with a 60-year-old man who had had a laryngectomy I outlined what we might do with regard to his learning an alternative way of producing voice and looking at the effects of the event on his life. He said that he was only interested in learning oesophageal speech and 'getting back to normal'. He had no wish to reflect on the implications of what had happened. He approached his task with great determination and achieved highly intelligible speech in a relatively short time. It was only when this was accomplished that he experienced quite deep depression. He realized that he could no longer pursue the hectic round of business meetings, conferences and financial dealings which he was used to. He suddenly felt that his life was over.

I had to some extent anticipated this as I listened to his plans for picking up the reins. I had got to know him as someone who could never do enough, never sit back and let the world go by. Although he had talked little about his personal life, I had come to understand something of the conflict he felt with regard to the demands of his job and his responsibilities to his wife and family. I asked him whether he was willing to share more of these feelings now and look at how he might lead a different kind of life, involving himself in activities he had had no time for before. He agreed to go away and write down all the things he might do and see whether there was 'another life to be lived'.

When the frenzy has to stop

I had negotiated four exploratory sessions with a mother and her 7-year-old son with a moderately severe articulation difficulty. His speech pattern was that of a much younger child. I had been told that he slept very little and had terrifying nightmares. While clearly concerned about him, mother complained of his tantrums and his lying. The sessions turned out to be stormy. Apart from assessing the child's speech I gained some understanding of his extreme anxiety and of the difficulties between himself and his mother. He was never still for a moment. He drew some very angry pictures, in which he was mainly fighting with monsters or grimacing hideously. When faced with anything new he threw it aside or sulked, his mother protesting that he should stop being silly and try. A recurring theme in his nightmares was of being chased by 'a beast on fire' and failing to reach a place of safety.

My strongest impression was that both of them were exhausted. When I asked for a picture of their day-to-day lives I found that mother worked part-time, had another younger child and was often on her own while her husband travelled on business. The child attended a very success-orientated school, was already given homework to do, went to karate, riding lessons, cubs and was learning to play the piano. He was competitive and both his parents were ambitious for him. They were disturbed by his speech difficulty and inclined to think that he could 'sort it out' if he wanted to.

I put it to mother that it was pointless trying to correct his speech at this stage. While his parents obviously wanted him to have every opportunity, he was trying to accomplish too much and was deeply stressed as a result. I offered to work with the child to reduce his anxiety, help him manage the nightmares and the explosions of temper. At the same time the mother and I would meet to talk through her own distress. At first she was hesitant, saying that she ought to be able to manage her child's difficulties herself. Then she acknowledged that her own childhood had been very unhappy and she had often wished her mother had sought help.

Beginning relationships

Underlying the work done in early sessions with these four people was the establishment of relationship. The girl who stuttered needed time not only to clarify the nature of the changes she felt she had to make but to experience for the first time what it was like to share her feelings with someone else. I had to learn the extent of the threat that exposure to others posed for her and understand how much it would cost her to let go of the negative theories about herself which had governed her life so far. Any small move on her part would need validation. Any insensitivity on my part could break the slender thread of trust.

The 60-year-old man saw me at first as an efficient technician who could teach him to speak again. If I had tried to persuade him to confront his feelings of loss at that stage he would have given me short shrift. Gradually, however, as he spoke a little more about his concern for his family, he allowed the relationship to become more human. By the time the realization of the implications of his loss of voice came home to him he was able to express his despair. This made it possible for me to focus on more personal issues and, by using the understanding of his need to be actively engaged in life, be alongside him in his mourning what he had lost and help him to focus his energy on building something new.

During his frenzied drawing and climbing all over the furniture, the child was, among other things, testing me out. I felt that he was checking to see whether I was strict, like his teacher, of whom he was afraid, or explosive like his mother. Although I did lift him down when he stood on top of the computer I remained steadfastly unshockable in the face of his drawings. I probably ended up as being classed with his paternal grandmother, with whom he was apparently at his most relaxed. His mother had probably needed someone to talk to for a long time. Although she felt guilty at 'not coping' it was possible to affirm that she had a great deal to handle, mostly on her own, and that she deserved something for herself.

Summary

This chapter has focused on the processes involved in the first stage of counselling. The nature of the referral has been shown to be especially important in the context of working with people with communication problems. The possible involvement of others besides the client and the need to establish a range of channels for mutual understanding have been stressed. In most approaches to counselling an initial period is negotiated, where the presenting problem is explored and the people involved have an opportunity to get to know each other. In this area, such a period is essential and there is even more for the counsellor to take into account before he or she can offer a course of action. Some examples have been given of how initial goals have been set up.

The following chapter looks at aspects of the counselling process over time. With communication being so central a part of the personality, the effects of change on the clients' perception of self will be discussed. The need for them to be aware of the effects of these changes on others will also be addressed.

5

The Counselling Process over Time

It will be clear from the previous chapter that a counsellor involved in working with people with communication problems has to keep track of a number of interweaving processes. As with a series of meetings with any client, development in relation to the presenting problem needs to be projected and traced as well as changes in the clients' perceptions of themselves and their worlds as a whole. With some of these particular clients, as has been indicated, it may not be possible to ameliorate the presenting problem substantially, but counselling can contribute to the maintenance of a sense of self and to the quality of life.

As any counselling relationship develops, transference and countertransference issues may emerge which could usefully be addressed. Here, we are sometimes in relationship with more than one person and must be aware of changes in interaction between all concerned. A child who feels misunderstood by adults will all too easily see the counsellor as the 'good' mother or father and project all the 'bad' onto the parents. A spouse may feel hurt and shut out if an older client seems to turn to the counsellor for what he or she is unable to give them. It is part of the clinician's task, when directly involved with other members, to enhance communication within families and thus help relationships to grow or to be healed.

One essential element of the first phase of work described in Chapter 4 was the establishment of appropriate means of communication for each client. As the series goes on, greater awareness of less accessible material, such as that found in dreams, memories or sheer gut feelings bring into play channels of perception that are often neglected. Even those with no language impairment but unused to expressing the complexities of personal experience may take time to develop the ability to convey their meanings. With some clients, inventive ways will need to be found for exchanging and making sense of such material. For example, a child may first express feelings and fantasies through the sounds of a musical instrument. Drawing or manipulating objects could emerge as preferred means of sharing states of mind for them and for adults with acquired difficulties. Only later, perhaps, will it be possible to verbalize what is going on for them.

Patterns of change

Such developments can be monitored over time. If we return to the point at which initial aims have been negotiated, the counsellor will not at this stage be able to foretell the final outcome, but should, from his or her understanding of the client so far, be able to help plan appropriate experiments for change. These will be based on where the client is now, be mindful of the possible implications of any movement and yet ready to tap the resources that have emerged.

Coming to know others

Many clients in all areas of counselling have difficulty in relating to others. Someone with a communication problem is even more at risk here. Shut in on themselves, one important focus of a series is often the development of not just 'social skills' but the ability to recognize ways of being that are different from their own, rather than simply alien. There are many ways of approaching this. I asked the young woman referred to in the last chapter as trying all her life to hide her dysfluency to write short sketches of some of the people she had to deal with at work and then consider what more she would need to understand about them in order to trust them with anything of herself. Another client drew a picture of his work situation in which a row of identical threatening faces stared at a figure representing himself. Both clients were asked to listen and observe in order to distinguish more individual differences. In both cases, this change of focus from themselves on to others in itself relieved some of the self-conscious anxiety.

When the client has begun to have a fuller sense of what another person is like, role-play can be a useful means of seeing things from others' points of view. First, the counsellor represents the other person and the client him- or herself. Then, by reversing the roles, the client may achieve surprising insights into what it feels like to be someone else. When the client is willing to communicate more openly with others who have been made less threatening through these means he or she can challenge old theories about the hostility or rejection that has always been anticipated.

Becoming oneself

Even relatively small changes in the way people communicate can have an effect both on the way they see themselves and the ways in which others respond to them. Children whose pattern of articulation is delayed may be emotionally quite mature but their speech will often cause others, especially adults, to interact with them as if they were younger. This in turn may elicit responses appropriate to that level and so a pattern of behaviour is set up between the children and their world. A lisp (or interdental 's') tends to be dismissed as a trivial feature of speech, but it can have quite damaging effects. It may be considered 'sweet' in a young girl but lead to a young woman not being taken seriously.

One 17-year-old, wanting to go to college with a new image of herself as 'grown up' worked very hard to correct the sound but found it difficult to transfer the change into conversation with her father – in fact with all men. When asked to be aware of how she was in a variety of social situations she had to acknowledge that she behaved differently in a number of ways when talking to men as opposed to women. She described herself with horror as 'simpering' and it took a good deal of work on her attitude to men and their's to her before she could be as she wanted to be and speak as she wanted to speak.

Trying to make changes in voice quality can also uncover confusion. The problem for young males with mutational voice disorders was referred to in Chapter 1. They, along with young people with dysphonias of various kinds, may be ambivalent about sounding 'different' and unsure as to what 'the real me' should sound like. They need time to adjust to a gradual change in self-presentation. An adult woman who has had a husky or 'ginny' voice for years may well have adopted other behaviours too which lead those around her to see her as 'one of the boys'. This may not be what she feels to be her true personality but it will take more than good vocal hygiene to change perceptions of her radically.

Given the need in such situations to address more than a single aspect of communication, Kelly's fixed-role therapy (1955: Ch. 8) would seem potentially useful. Using this approach a sketch is drawn up, with the client's cooperation, of a person in some ways similar to him- or herself but different enough to allow for experiment with a range of new behaviours, including the change in articulation or voice quality, once it is possible to produce them in sessions. The client is asked to take on this character for a time, reporting back to the counsellor to discuss any difficulties. Although, as stipulated, clients cease to be this other person after the experimental period, the experience of communicating in a new way in a context divorced from other old unwanted patterns could give them a greater sense of choice and confidence.

Allowing another to be

In all the examples given above, the perceptions and responses of other people play their part both in setting up particular patterns of interaction and in the ease or difficulty with which a client can make changes. With young children and especially those more severely handicapped, the onus for change may be on the parents or caretakers. A child may improve in speech and language skills and there will be work to be done to maintain that improvement. But the focus for the counsellor will be on helping the child to develop a growing sense of self *besides* being someone with a handicap. Many parents of such children encourage them to take as full a part as possible in life and make only the necessary distinctions between their needs and those of siblings. Others, however, continue to construe the children largely in terms of the disabilities and set them apart from others in the family. The counsellor must find ways of widening this narrow focus, which can have negative effects on all concerned.

It is often the parents' unresolved grief that needs to be addressed and their sense of being responsible and even punished for their child's condition. A mother who refuses to allow anyone else to look after her disabled child so that she can have respite from the demands imposed not only traps herself but gives her child little chance to learn independently or experience a range of relationships. However, through a series of small experiments, leaving the child with others for gradually increasing periods, she can come to lessen her desperate anxiety. The counsellor meanwhile may explore with her the issues surrounding her feelings for the child.

A similar reluctance to accept help can be found where one partner in a marriage suffers a stroke. When impaired communication is involved the spouse may not only take over the physical management of the disabled person but also speak for them, interpret thoughts and feelings to others, thus forming a barrier between the disabled spouse and the rest of the world. Alternatively, the able spouse may look eveywhere for a 'cure' and demand 'treatment' from many sources, rejecting one form after another as not producing results: for example, the disabled partner *must* be taught to speak/walk again whatever the cost. In either situation, the counsellor/clinician, having undertaken the early sessions of assessment and evaluated what might be possible over time, will best present the couple with a clear programme of work which addresses the communication needs of the client and the psychological needs of both parties.

The partner who has 'taken over' should continue to feel that his or her help is invaluable, while coming to understand the importance of the client doing as much for him- or herself as possible. Observing the counsellor giving the client time to communicate in a number of different ways should encourage the partner to do the same – and space to be. This may then allow the partner to attend to his or her own needs. Those who have gone from 'expert' to 'expert', looking for a cure, may not listen to the counsellor either when he or she gives them an understanding of what can be done. But if the counsellor demonstrates an understanding of what lies behind their desperation they may, at last, come to rest and begin to work for achievable goals. In my experience, there is relief as well as sadness when denial gives way to acceptance. The work for achievable goals may be slow and limited, but alongside it we would hope for a development in both of a new understanding of themselves as they come to terms with their changed situation.

Spreading dependencies
The theme of dependency has run through all of the patterns of change discussed so far. A person who seeks to move out of isolation into relationships with others is recognizing the need to be able to rely on others. Someone who no longer wishes to be stuck in a child-like pattern of interaction due to immature speech or voice is taking the risk of reciprocal dependency. Letting go, where a child or handicapped adult has had only you to turn to, acknowledges that a dispersal of dependencies is healthier for all concerned.

The issue of dependence/independence is a crucial one for many clients and for some with communication problems it forms a governing factor in their lives. The notion of spreading dependencies may be hard to entertain and a polarized position is taken up. Some young people who stutter, for example, come to look to their mothers to speak for them – to answer the telephone, go into shops for them, protect them from exposure. They may take this reliance into later life – choosing work where there is little need to speak, a partner who is willing to do all the talking. Such dependency goes deeper than speech and is usually associated with general passivity. In contrast, of course, there are others who are determined to speak for themselves, infuriated if anyone finishes a sentence for them, and would rather lose out altogether than ask for help.

The counsellor's task in the former situation of 'learned helplessness' is an extremely difficult one. I have to confess that unless such people have reason to be dissatisfied with a life-long dependent position I have not yet found ways of reducing the threat of a real change on this dimension. Sometimes, however, the dependency is less widespread and areas may be found where they are willing and able to stand on their own feet. Someone who concedes all conversation to a partner when in company may speak up at work or when responsible for children. Through role-play of each situation the different attitudes and feelings experienced may be explored and a transfer of behaviours experimented with. (We shall be discussing later the implications of such changes for others later in the book.)

One of the most painful aspects of the experience of losing communication skills is the inevitable need to rely on others. A person who becomes dysphasic or whose speech is rendered unintelligible will often also have physical disabilities. The counsellor will need to acknowledge feelings of resentment in some and understand others who, for a while at least, give up in despair. The plans made to assist during the exploratory phase should be presented with care and respect, allowing the person to reject them for the time being if feeling too angry or depressed to respond. The establishment of a relationship, where each comes to know the other through sharing experiences which do not have to do with speech, will often form the basis for more direct work. The counsellor will learn what is truly meaningful for the client and he or she will gradually set the agenda and choose the focus of sessions.

Whatever the client's difficulties, one aim will be to find a balance in terms of dependency. Kelly (1969) describes an optimum situation where a mature person knows to whom to turn for what and when to rely on the self. So-called 'independence training' for handicapped children has proved ineffective, as the aim is to make a sharp change from one extreme to the other. When the course is over they and their families go back to their old ways of dealing with things. Where we find polarization in over-reliance on others or refusal to accept help we would hope to work out a *dispersal* of dependency which allows the person to achieve the most they can by using a range of people or agencies to supply their needs. And this applies to carers as well as to the verbally impaired. This may involve work on the development of trust in others and the growth of confidence in the person's own untapped resources. Above all, the counsellor must be sensitive to what the clients' most urgent needs *are*, rather than pre-empt them in the light of what *seems* important.

Widening horizons

As clients become able to form networks of new dependency and relationships with a wider range of people they are also in a position to widen their range of activity beyond what they may have felt possible. Many people who stutter have avoided work which would involve speaking in a group. They may also have regarded joining any kind of club or association as out of the question, even though they have the skills and interests which these bodies cater for. One man who was an excellent golfer had delayed joining his local club for years because he would have to give his name when he enquired about joining. A woman with an excellent soprano voice longed to sing with others but dreaded the 'conversation' that would occur during breaks in practices.

These are examples of the kind of constriction in the person's perception of things, where only the verbal aspects of a situation are considered. The counsellor can help clients to widen their view by asking them to picture the *whole*, to consider the many aspects of a situation and to recognize that, to others, the quality of their speech is not of primary importance. The singer referred to above found that it was her singing and her knowledge of music that interested others. The golfer was asked his handicap as often as he was asked his name. An older man whose speech was very difficult to understand was warmly welcomed when he approached a children's association, offering them his skill in making and repairing dolls. In all three instances, acceptance by others led to an improvement in communication itself as they grew more confident to experiment.

Changing perception

One kind of change in perception has already been touched on in the examples of people anticipating situations from a broader viewpoint. Others involve: challenging old theories, particularly in relation to the presenting problem; revising expectations of what overcoming the problem will bring; and, most important of all perhaps, re-evaluating other aspects of the self besides that which has been causing all the trouble.

Challenging old theories

It has been said throughout that people will have theories about their difficulties and that these must be respected and taken into account when the counsellor considers measures for alleviating them. Sometimes, however, it is the theories themselves that are a barrier to progress and unless they can be modified or, eventually, replaced altogether, changes that are possible in the clinical situation will not transfer to life outside.

In Dalton and Dunnett (1992) we looked at some of the personal theories people hold and how they may affect their ability to change. A person who sets great store by heredity, for example, may feel doomed by the fact that his father and grandfather stuttered all their lives. Someone who sees a crucial early relationship as the cause of all her ills may need to go on losing her voice whenever feeling criticized by such a figure. The third generation stutterer can be helped to question the inevitability of taking after his forebears by considering not only the many differences between himself and them but the new ways of approaching the problem that have been developed since their day. It will be more difficult, perhaps, for the dysphonic woman to move from her position as victim. But through work on taking responsibility for her own actions and finding the advantages of having personal choice she may be able to free herself from this most limiting of situations.

Parents who see 'having a handicap' as in some way casting disgrace on them will pass on such a notion to their child with a disability. The counsellor will need both to increase the child's self-esteem, through validation of efforts to overcome difficulties and to attempt to loosen the parents' intense focus on their supposed public image. This will undoubtedly also entail attention to their own self-confidence. Reference was made in Chapter 3 (page 31) to people who feel that they have brought their problem on themselves in some way. This may sap their motivation to overcome it. We need to explore with them their propensity for guilt and, very likely, help them to move out of the depression that underlies it. Only then will they be able to acknowledge that 'deserving' has little to do with what happens to people and that it is what you make of things that expresses who you are.

Revising expectations

Some clients enter counselling with only a vague wish to feel better. Others come with clear ideas as to the changes they expect. Clients with a long-term difficulty such as stuttering or chronic dysphonia may see their lives as being transformed by 'a cure'. Like many with eating disorders, they will dream of conquering the world or becoming irresistible. We should, of course, have uncovered such dreams during the early stage of counselling. But revising them in the direction of reality may take time. One way of preserving such illusions is not to make progress. Then the 'if only . . .' can remain intact. If, however, experiments for change are planned carefully and their outcomes evaluated with sensitivity as well as honesty, the revision of expectations will be a gradual and less shocking process.

It is important when working with those who have acquired disorders due to brain damage that we prepare them for less than complete recovery, without dashing all hope. No one can foretell from the beginning how far a person may progress in restoring speech and language function. After a time, however, it may be clear that the person will remain quite severely impaired. Some clients and their relatives realize this. Others go on hoping for much greater recovery than is possible. Our best approach is to focus as much as possible on the present and the fullest use of communicative ability as it exists. We must make sure that there is no undue pressure on the client to achieve beyond his or her capacity. We will hope also to help his relatives take pressure off themselves and put their energy into building a new life-style which will suit their changed situation.

Similarly, it is painful to have to tell the parents of a child that only limited progress can be made because of the impairment which underlies the disability. However, using Enderby's four levels of perspective referred to in Chapter 3 (page 38), we can help them to focus, as we do, on reducing the handicap experienced through the disability. Meeting with other parents can be beneficial here and seeing what use they make of alternative means of communication, say, or how they get round specific aspects of a problem. The revision of expectations is often made easier by sharing them with others in the same situation.

The self as a whole person

Building a view of the self around a problem, be it communicative or otherwise, is all too common. A girl may feel bulimic and nothing but bulimic, an anxious person nothing but anxiety. This kind of self-perception often starts in childhood. Mother is concerned about her daughter's eating and food soon becomes a battle ground for the whole family. A boy quickly acquires a reputation as 'nervous' or 'shy' and has little alternative but to live up to it. Parents who have a child with a physical or learning difficulty are naturally very concerned but through their efforts to help, even their exaggerated praise at any small achievement they may constrict the child's own experience of self.

As has been implied, the lives of many people who stutter are governed by their dysfluency and by the anticipation of situations largely in terms of the speech involved. And this can be so even where overt dysfluency is rare. Self-characterizations (see Chapter 2, page 21) will often reveal such preoccupation. Asking the person to write about themselves in terms of 'Who am I apart from my stutter?' may be the first step towards elaborating a fuller picture of the self. One young man was asked what three things important people in his life might say about him. He included 'He stutters' for all of them. Then he checked this out by asking the people themselves. Not one of them referred to his speech and he realized from studying their responses that they all chose attributes that were important to *them*: his humour, his quick temper and his skill in athletics. His dysfluency did not immediately become unimportant to *him*, but the exercise did help him to look at himself more as a whole.

If a counsellor working with a client with a communication problem focuses largely on the difficulties surrounding it, he or she too will be contributing to a limited self-perception. Where the range of concern is widened to encompass the ways in which the client experiences life in many dimensions, such constriction can be loosened. A woman whose articulation was impaired by nerve damage after an accident was at first obsessed by the effect she felt it had on her relationship with her two young children. She could no longer read or 'explain things' to them. She was also upset in case people thought her slurred speech meant that she was drunk. When we went through her day, however, it was clear that she managed her children extremely well and provided a great deal of enjoyment for them. She also agreed to tell people why her speech was slurred when this was appropriate. She found that this 'got it out of the way' and enabled her to relate to them with less embarrassment. Most of our sessions were then focused on issues to do with her religious faith, which was very important to her.

The effects of change on others

One thing which both counsellor and client must be aware of throughout the series is the possible effects of change on others. (I am not here referring to the devastating impact of sudden change shared by adults with acquired disorders and their families. That, of course, will be of concern.) Where someone who has been known only by a partner, say, as quite dysfluent, patterns of communication may have been set up between them, with the partner speaking for him or her, 'taking charge' in restaurants, perhaps, or even bearing the brunt of ticking off the children. If increased fluency is to be maintained old patterns of dependency will need to change with it. It is important for the counsellor to anticipate the effects of the client's assuming greater responsibility.

He or she will probably need to negotiate with some sensitivity if hurt and confusion are to be avoided.

Changes in voice quality, as we have said, can be difficult to come to terms with, even where, in theory, they are for the better. It is of no help to clients if they are responded to as if they are not themselves. They too may need to prepare others for the difference. In most families, progress in a child's language or speech will be welcomed and encouraged. But, again, siblings are not always ready for the client to seize the conversational ball when they have been used to having a quiet brother or sister. They may, in fact, impede progress if he or she is not given time and space to develop the growing use of skills in everyday life.

Resistance to change

Fransella (1993) points out that 'resistance' is generally regarded as an obstacle to be overcome in many approaches to psychotherapy and counselling. There is a notion of failure on the part of the client. She refutes this idea, quoting Neimeyer (1986: 248): 'labelling a client as "resistant" can be more destructive than clarifying, insofar as it offers a pseudo-explanation for his failure to show therapeutic movement and implies an adversarial relationship between client and therapist'. Given that the counselling relationship, from the more client-centred approaches at least, is viewed as a partnership, with both parties engaged in addressing the same problem, it seems more useful to look at what is happening in terms of a difference between how the client sees the problem and how the counsellor sees it. It is for the counsellor to try to understand why what he or she thinks *ought* to occur does not.

It seems obvious that someone who has been isolated due to a communication problem *must* benefit from developing relationships with others. Yet the experiments planned to bring this about are either 'forgotten' or somehow always go wrong. We can refer glumly to 'sabotage' or take another look at how the person has conducted his or her life so far and what the benefits are of remaining self-contained although able to converse more freely when wished. We may see the potential for greater self-development where someone is able to speak or vocalize in a more mature way. The client has not 'failed' if he or she does not follow this path, but has *chosen* to go on living in the same way. We have not sufficiently explored the implications of change for the particular person. Our goals are inappropriate.

I referred earlier to helping clients to discover what else they are besides 'stutterers', 'brain damaged', or 'dysphonic'. I had a bee in my bonnet some years ago about dysfluent people needing to construe themselves as 'people who sometimes stuttered', rather than as 'stutterers'. This was fine for some clients, especially the young. But for others it was simply too huge a shift in self-perception and probably got in the way. It was much more validating for a life-long stutterer to keep that very central part of the sense of self and learn to cope with things regardless. I was attempting to bring about change at what Kelly would call a 'core' level when what proved acceptable and manageable for clients was change at a behavioural level parallel with a growth of confidence and self-esteem.

Lack of change in an initially hoped-for direction need not mean 'failure' on the part of either client or counsellor. As the counselling series proceeds the circumstances and needs of the client may change and both counsellor and client must be responsive to this.

Revision of goals

In Chapter 4 setting initial goals in the light of the early, exploratory sessions was discussed. Since no counsellor would claim to foretell the outcome of later work with clients it is expected that these initial aims will be modified as time goes on. Where direct work on voice, language, articulation or fluency is undertaken alongside psychological intervention the emphasis may shift from one to the other. Often, the client seeks behavioural change most urgently and only when the implications of the effects of new behaviour emerge will he or she bring more psychological issues to the sessions. The young woman referred to as wanting to correct a lisp had anticipated mainly working on articulation but, once she had achieved the more acceptable 's' sound in the sessions but failed to transfer it to communication with men, felt that she wanted to review her relationship with her father and with men in general.

Working with young children with speech and language difficulties always involves revision of goals as progress cannot be predicted accurately. Although, as has been said, we will have tried to prepare the parents for a range of outcomes it may be hard for them to accept that their child's full potential is less than they had hoped. The focus of our counselling work with them will often widen from an emphasis on the child to include issues of their own feelings and fears for the future.

The mother of a 7-year-old boy with a severe stutter hoped that the problem could be overcome through 'exercises'. When I asked her to take steps to modify the child's speaking environment she was more than willing to make changes in her own management of him. But she avoided reference to her relationship with her husband for some time. When she saw, however, that tensions between them clearly affected the child she agreed to come on her own to talk things through. From then on the child was no longer the direct focus of concern. Her husband joined us and I saw the boy occasionally to monitor the effects of changes in them on his speech.

Sometimes, sadly, aims have to change because the client concerned has a deteriorating condition. If this is known from the beginning the counsellor will be careful to set short-term goals and focus what takes place very much in the present. A man with Parkinson's Disease was still able to work when I first met him and our sessions had the combined purpose of maintaining an appropriate rate of speech and volume of voice and addressing his feelings about becoming ill. He ranged through anger with God for letting it happen to guilt about letting down his wife and family. By the time he had to give up his job it was a struggle to speak intelligibly. He wanted, however, to continue the sessions. Although far from reconciled to his fate, he was able to accept that his family and friends accepted him and simply wanted him with them for as long as possible.

Summary

In this chapter some of the patterns of change often occuring in work with people with communication problems have been described. Issues around so-called resistance to change have been addressed and the need for revision of initial aims. In Chapter 6, concerned with the ending of counselling, the importance of developing strategies to ensure the maintenance and continuance of change will be stressed.

6

Ending Counselling: towards Continuing Change

It should be clear from previous chapters that the wide range of aims set up in working with people with communication problems will call for a range of endings to the counselling process. In the case of a child with delayed speech and language, for example, the counsellor/clinician will attempt both to enhance the young person's communication skills and to prevent or ameliorate any effects on his or her psychological and social growth. At the same time, the parents, without whose understanding and cooperation professional help will be ineffective, may need to be supported in their ongoing task of facilitating their child's optimum development. The end of counselling here will be determined as much by their confidence in their ability to handle all aspects of the situation as in the young person's measurable progress.

In many other instances, as with most clients, goals will have been set and reviewed as the series proceeds and the end of counselling will be related to the achievement of those goals. The counsellor will hope to have helped the client to develop strategies for handling old difficulties and an experimental attitude which will enable the client to invent means for dealing with new ones in the future. Where behaviour change is sought, as with dysfluency or dysphonia, the client's initial aims may prove unattainable, but psychological intervention should enable the development of a sense of self as an effectively functioning person, who will continue to learn and grow after the series ends.

As has been said already, clients with acquired speech and language disorders may reach only a limited level of restoration. Throughout the series, one aim will have been to make the most of whatever abilities can be retrieved and whatever alternative means of communication prove useful. Along with this, the counsellor will try to help the client to work through the loss that has been suffered and to restore a sense of self. The end of counselling may be signalled by the client's more confident communication with others, together with the development of a new life-style. Group work may already be a part of the rehabilitation programme or a natural step on from individual work.

In Chapter 5 it was said that where someone has a deteriorating condition the focus needs to be very much in the present. Some clients will want to share their fears for the future, others will not, but the counsellor's 'professional' knowledge of the situation may make him or her easier to share with than people within the family. One couple spoke separately of the man's dying for some time before they were able to face it together. Although it is not always possible within the NHS to continue support until the end, most clinicians would want to be there for clients until they themselves chose to finish. A colleague who works extensively with people who have had a laryngectomy sees her relationship with them as being 'for life'. She works with them individually and then they join a group for as long as they wish or are able to attend. This is clearly a different situation from those described earlier and requires a different approach.

Reflecting on initial goals

In most counselling situations the time for ending will be planned ahead to enable those concerned to look at the series as a whole, reflect on what has occurred and anticipate the future. Often, clients spontaneously make comparisons with how they were and how they are now. But to go back to the beginning and consider the issues brought to the first meeting, recall expectations and apprehensions can be a useful experience.

Neither I nor the mother with impaired articulation referred to in the last chapter, whose main preoccupation when she came was communication with her children, anticipated that we would spend many of the ten sessions we had discussing her religious faith. But this had been important, since her doubts about her mothering were closely linked with her belief that the accident had in some way made her less fit to carry out what she saw as God's purpose for her. The young woman with a lisp had wanted to 'sound grown-up' and thus be treated as an adult, but here too our aims needed to embrace more: her perceptions of men and her relationships with them.

These and other examples suggest that although behaviour change may be uppermost in the client's mind when beginning counselling, whether direct work is expected or not, change at a psychological level is inevitably bound up with it. As we shall see in Chapter 7, there is great controversy in the area of stuttering between those who see behaviour modification as the key to success and those who believe that psychological intervention is an essential part of treatment. The former do not deny that attitude change 'happens' as a result of increased fluency, but they see no need for the clinician to do anything about it. In my experience and those of many colleagues, while clients may begin work with a behavioural focus they will themselves introduce psychological issues as time goes on. Looking back towards the end of the series will enable the client to view how and why the focus of the work changed.

Assessing changes in perception

Much of the counsellor and client's review of what they have done together will take place through conversation. (By 'client' in this context I refer both to those with communication problems and any members of the families involved.) There are, however, a number of other ways in which change can be assessed and these are discussed in this section.

Repertory grid technique

Personal construct counsellors are not the only ones who use Kelly's repertory grid technique (1955) to gauge changes in perception of the self and others (e.g. Ryle, 1985). The technique was described briefly in Chapter 2 and an example is given in Chapter 8. If a client completes a grid early on in the series and then again towards the end, it is possible to see whether desired changes have taken place. Comparison between the two grids will also show whether initial aims themselves have changed. One young man who saw himself as 'not achieving' and rated 'Me as I'd like to be' at the extreme end of its opposite, 'successful', had changed his mind a year later when the implications of becoming like his 'workaholic' brother had been reflected on. Where there is less distinction made between the 'self now' and 'me as I'd like to be' in the second grid the person demonstrates a more positive self-image.

Self characterizations

An initial self-characterization was described in Chapter 2 and an example can be found in Chapter 7. Writing of this kind may be used throughout the counselling series (see Fransella, 1981). As part of the review leading up to the end it can be very useful. A client could be asked to compare how he or she felt at the beginning and now or simply to write another self-description without reference to the first, so that comparisons may be made.

Changes in self-perception, again, will be looked for. A shift in emphasis from preoccupation with the presenting problem to a range of life issues will suggest a widening of view. The introduction of reference to other people and more activities imply a fuller life. One young woman's first self-characterization dwelt mainly on her early years and her relationship with her mother. By the end her concern was much more with the present and what was to come.

Other channels of self-expression

With or without language impairment, some people express change more vividly through drawing or other non-verbal means. Drawing is the most commonly used alternative form of expression. A client whose moods changed sharply from day to day began each session by drawing how he felt. Using simple 'stick' figures and a few details, such as a heavy weight on his chest as he lay prone or a bird flying through a window, he conveyed his current state of being very clearly. During our penultimate session we looked through the drawings in sequence. There were variations and swings but the overall trend was towards less frenzy and a greater sense of containment.

A 7-year-old boy was described in Chapter 4 as producing drawings of hideous monsters and having nightmares in which he was being chased by a beast on fire. We worked on his dreaming by 'making up' dreams where he directed their course himself. He introduced his dog at one stage to help him fight off the beast. Thereafter 'Toby' did appear in his dreams. His final drawing at our last regular meeting was of himself and Toby routing a rather pathetic-looking creature. (I was interested to read recently in Cushway and Sewell's (1993) book on counselling with dreams and nightmares that this is a well-tried method for helping people with troublesome dreams.)

Clients sometimes produce their own forms of self-representation quite spontaneously. A colleague worked with a woman who was a potter. When the time came to end counselling she produced a piece of work showing how she saw herself when the series started, as it progressed and currently. From a rough round base three heads emerged: one bowed with eyes closed, one partly raised but drawn and tense, the third turning upwards with a hand cupping the mouth as she called out to the world. Lacking such skill, a client of mine chose two objects in my room to express the contrast she felt between herself when she first came and towards the end of our sessions. The first was a stiff rather conventional bland-faced doll. The second a scruffy rag-doll with the face of a clown. The important thing to her was the looseness of the clown's body and his ability to stand up to the roughest of handling.

Difficulties in maintaining change

Whatever the presenting problem, no counselling series should end without those concerned addressing the issue of 'relapse'. With some difficulties, such as eating disorders, drug abuse, alcoholism and, in our particular area, dysfluency and dysphonia, a return to old behaviours will be obvious. However, the client may take some time to acknowledge what is happening. Behind the regression in behaviour there is a more crucial return to old ways of perceiving the self and one's world.

One-dimensional change

As Hayhow and Levy (1989: 170) point out: 'Most frequently relapse can be explained by the superficial nature of the changes that have been made.' They are referring to a change from stuttering to fluency through the learning of fluency skills which is not accompanied by lasting changes in self-perception and in the person's internal approach to speaking situations which have always been troublesome. But superficial change can occur in any counselling situation. In the first flush of hope when normal voice is attained or restored client and counsellor may rejoice too soon that the goal has been achieved. Without the test of time and exposure to old pressures, however, new behaviour may be short-lived.

Communicative challenge

Perhaps the greatest pressure comes from feeling ill-equipped to tackle a widening range of communication situations. If the client has held back, due to lack of language or speech skill or voice, he or she may simply not know how to respond to the greater demands now being imposed. Clients may have been helped more than they realized, with others being careful not to interrupt, giving them time to speak. After a while, perhaps, clients are exposed to more stress in their 'improved' state than they were when the difficulty was more apparent. Anxiety can adversely affect any aspect of communication, from encoding the language needed to express oneself to producing the voice which will carry that language.

Changes in self-perception

More threatening than the greater demands which come with progress may be the extent to which the client has to modify views of the self. For a while, behaving in more assertive ways and being seen by others as having a contribution to make will feel great. If, however, confidence has not been allowed to grow steadily through gradually testing out new possibilites, the person may be too easily thrown by confrontation or unexpected responses. It will feel more comfortable to retreat to the 'safety' of shyness or self-deprecation. For someone with an acquired impairment to create a new way of being and communicating, time and opportunities for validation will be needed. There is the danger of a return to initial feelings of helplessness and despair if these do not remain available.

Preparing for continuing change

When we near the end of a counselling series it is not enough simply to be aware of what difficulties there may be in maintaining changes in behaviour and perception. The concept of 'maintaining' change is, as Hayhow and Levy (1989) point out, a limiting one. In the literature on stuttering 'maintenance of fluency' has become *the* vexed topic. However, Hayhow and Levy reject such terminology out of hand as it implies 'keeping things the same, as if there were a universal end-product to the process of stuttering therapy' (1989: 170). And the same applies to any experience of counselling. The client may feel that certain goals have been reached but he or she should also have a sense that what has been achieved is only part of a process of development which will continue long after the sessions have ended. We need, therefore, not only to prepare for the challenges described in the previous section but also to anticipate further changes that life may call for.

Anticipating challenge

Some children who have ventured into fuller communication with their world through developing language or articulation skills, fluency or normal voice, may well move on in parallel with their peers to meet the demands of an expanding life. For others, however, it may be felt that, for example, moving to a senior school will bring pressures for which they might not be prepared. If such a move is some way off, a break in sessions may be appropriate, to be resumed nearer the time. If, however, it is pending, it will be important for the child and carers to anticipate new challenges.

If we ask children to write or tell us what things will be like at the new school, we can note what their priorities are. Are they worried about the work or concerned about friends? How do they imagine a school day will be compared with the structure they are used to? One 11-year-old girl was most anxious about getting lost in the new building and, having had some negative experiences of teachers, wondered how strict her new form teacher would be. Her parents, on the other hand, who had also been asked to write of their expectations, focused largely on whether she would keep up with the others academically. In this case, as often, it was possible to visit the school and at least gain some idea of what was to come. Measures were taken to ensure that she would have extra help with language if needed and she was introduced to two children who would be in her class and 'befriend' her.

Similar challenges in the expansion of their educational setting are met by young adults. Loss of the structure provided by school life is welcomed by many but for some the transition to college or university may be bewildering. Where the counsellor has understood that a young person in this situation has difficulty meeting new people and adapting to new ways it is essential that help is given to prepare him or her for the many differences that will be encountered. In one instance, the last few sessions were largely given over to role-play of imaginary situations, both 'tutorial' and social. The young man made some plans for joining the rowing and chess clubs – activities in which he had some skill and therefore would be able to contribute something, rather than having to present himself in purely social terms at the beginning.

Crucial life events

Changing schools and going on to higher education are often in themselves crucial life events, which may take people forward or bring set-backs if they are not sufficiently prepared to test out their newly-developed communication abilities and self-perceptions. Getting a first job or returning to work after illness can be even more challenging. In some cases it will be appropriate not to end counselling until the transition is made. In others, again, anticipation of possible stress factors will form part of the final phase. Issues such as whether to tell people at work, for example, that the telephone may cause problems or paperwork may need extra time will need to be addressed. If someone's voice is vulnerable to strain, strategies to conserve it need to be worked out.

Less easy to anticipate will be the effects of events such as marriage or the birth of a child. A client who has had relationship problems in the past may have developed closer friendships and learned both to give of themselves and to receive validation from others. Forming a partnership will pose no greater challenge for them than for other people. It may be, however, that old difficulties arise with intimacy and old self-doubts re-emerge. It is not suggested that clients should hang on to the counsellor until they are sure that things will work out! But clients should feel free to return to look again at issues that they have explored before with someone who knows them well. A one-off session, with their previous experience behind it, may be enough to set them in motion again.

Some three years after the ending of counselling a young woman wrote to say that she had married and now had a baby and a 7-year-old stepdaughter. She had had moderate language difficulties and much of our work concerned her earlier sense of inadequacy in comparison with her academically bright sister. However, my client had made good progress and become much more self-assured. Now her stepdaughter, who resented her, had realized her problem and was making much of it. She also feared that her son might have 'inherited' her language difficulties. Although now I would explore such fears for future children, the advent of a stepchild could not have been foreseen. In a short period of further counselling we looked at the broader issues of the child's difficulties in accepting her, which were clearly not based only on her language problem.

It is not, of course, any counsellor's task to attempt to prepare clients for all of life's vicissitudes. However well we come to know another at a certain time in their lives, given that counselling plays only a small part in a person's development, it would be presumptuous to assume a knowledge of how they will deal with future events. From an understanding of the implications of particular communication problems, however, a counsellor/clinician may anticipate the effects of extreme anxiety or stress on particular clients. Without ending the series by looking forward to trouble, it may be important to touch on new demands which might come with new life events.

Termination, 'on review' or 'open door'?

It has been implied earlier in this chapter that there will be circumstances in which it will be important to arrange to see clients again at a later date – when a child is due to start a new school, for example. Where the person has a deteriorating condition, counselling may continue until the end. In other instances, the nature of the communication problem may call for breaks in the series to allow for changes to be assimilated before new areas are addressed. A fourth scenario cannot be ignored, however – that is, where counselling ends with no progress having been made.

'Resistance' revisited

In Chapter 5 resistance was discussed from the point of view of a proposed change being too threatening for clients, rather than any bloody-mindedness or failure on their part. In a book concerned with hard-earned lessons from counselling (Dryden, 1992), three of the examples discussed in my contribution quite clearly involved 'resistance' on the part of the client and a slowness on mine to recognize what was at stake for them. 'Tony', for instance, now in his early forties, had searched for a 'cure' for his stutter for more than twenty years. But nothing had 'worked' – none of the professionals had been able to help him. Locked in his theory of himself as the victim of his parents' mishandling, he could not afford to reach out for anything different. When we parted after five sessions he took with him yet more confirmation that he was right.

A colleague is currently working with the mother of a child with agenesis of the part of the brain essential to development of language and other cognitive abilities. Everyone involved knows that there is little hope of progress, but the mother insists that he understands, can speak some words and is improving. My colleague has tried to help her to acknowledge the extent of the child's difficulties so that appropriate provision can be made for him. But the mother cannot allow herself to believe that her child is severely handicapped and continues to try to find someone who will at last understand. Counselling, at this time, is useless to her.

A matter of timing

In less tragic circumstances it may be that the client can accomplish a good deal, but needs time to assimilate certain changes before embarking on new areas. Here there can be clear agreement as to the length of a break and the timing of the next phase. A young man with poor articulation worked for several months to improve his communication skills and, in the process, became much more able to put himself in others' shoes and understand many aspects of social interaction. He had a great deal to consolidate in terms of changes in his own behaviour and his confidence in himself needed time to grow further. We decided to have a break over the summer and resume in the autumn with a view to going more deeply into aspects of relationship with others.

A young woman came for help with recurrent dysphonia at a time when she hoped for promotion. In the course of our exploration of her voice problem we touched on some complex material related to childhood abuse. She realized that she needed to work on this more deeply, but with her job uppermost in her mind, we agreed that the process might be too disturbing and concentrated on issues of the present. She got her promotion and discontinued the sessions until she felt settled in her new post. It was some nine months later when she contacted me again and we resumed our work together.

Such breaks may occur in counselling with many clients. They are perhaps more likely where the person has to manage change at more than one level, as in these cases of communicative impairment.

On review

Keeping clients 'on review' might suggest that the counsellor is encouraging too much dependency. It should surely be left to adults to refer themselves back if they wish or parents to refer their children if they are concerned. In certain instances, however, it may be important to have agreed review points. This will mainly occur with children, especially where they have had difficulty with language at a young age and will have discontinued sessions with more development to come. Reassessment of language to make sure that they are not falling behind, together with an evaluation of how they are progressing socially and in terms of self-perception may prevent unnecessary neglect of later problems.

If a young child has been dysfluent he or she may not be seen unless there is obvious trouble, but it is important to make contact with the parents to check on progress, especially as they will be largely instrumental in continuing the process of change in their child. Whether the onus should be on the parents or on the clinician to keep in touch is a matter of debate. If review dates are fixed periodically there is no confusion.

When coming to the end of counselling it is important to anticipate the future. When working with people who stutter, one issue that needs to be addressed is a possible increase in dysfluency at some time. Some will take such an occurrence in their stride and have no need to refer to anyone else. Others may try to ignore what is happening and later wish that they had taken some action. If the person has achieved fluency or a substantial improvement in communication, disappointment will be great and they may be ashamed and unwilling to return for help, unless the possibility has been faced ahead of time. A pre-arranged review may serve to pick up reverses in both speech behaviour and attitude. In fact, a number of clients have felt that being *due* for review has drawn their attention to small but significant changes and enabled them to focus where they need to.

The 'open door'

An arrangement preferred by many counsellors and clients is that of leaving the door open, should clients wish to make contact at a later date. But even with such a loose agreement, the possible implications of a return should be anticipated. How might it feel? What might it mean in terms of the work that has been done? The counsellor needs to emphasize the point that future events and difficulties cannot be foreseen. We all regress to earlier ways of viewing ourselves and our worlds when under threat, however much we may have changed. We can become bogged down by old material which we thought we had 'dealt with'. Even a one-off session with someone who has worked with us through that old material can remind us of how we were able to see things differently. And, knowing that the counsellor has some under-standing of who we are and how we function, can prevent the depressing sense of being back to square one.

Sometimes a client expresses a wish to work again, but on something quite new. The communication problem which may have been the focus of the original sessions is no longer the problem. As a relationship has been established it is important for the counsellor to see the client and it may be quite appropriate for them continue. Where, however, the difficulty is one in which the counsellor has little or no experience this needs to be acknowl-edged and a referral to someone else will be preferable. As a counsellor working in other areas besides communication I have been referred several clients with eating disorders, for example, who have worked with speech and language therapy colleagues. Similarly, I have referred on clients who have come back wanting to tackle areas of difficulty which I feel unequipped to help them with. Having a network of colleagues with 'specialities' is a very useful part of the counsellor's armoury.

Saying 'goodbye'

How we conduct the final session with clients will depend very much on our understanding of each person. The work of sum-marizing the series and anticipating the future should already have been completed. Some clients like to have something written down to take away with them and the time may be spent on jointly composing what might prove useful in the future. Others may be feeling sad or apprehensive and such feelings will be given priority. A male client recently was shocked by what he felt. It was as if, he said, I had 'booted him out', which he knew was not true. We looked again at his experience of leaving home for boarding school and he decided that this was 'an old echo'.

Mearns (1993: 38) points to a danger which lurks towards the end of even a successful counselling process:

> Because our culture is bedevilled by fairytales whereby endings are not merely 'happy' but 'happy ever after', the client and indeed the counsellor may be shaken by the fact that the client is not feeling at all happy – indeed, he or she may be somewhat depressed. The client at the end of a successful counselling process will have *lost* a lot. He or she will have lost a set of assumptions and a self-concept which, although limiting of his or her existence, had also served to *define* that existence. This sense of loss may be intensified by the fact that the client had always presumed that once through this difficulty, life would be like the fairytales. (emphases in original)

The counsellor too has feelings about clients and there is nothing wrong with letting them know that working with them has meant something to you and taught you something. One woman with whom I had had great difficulty in the early stages wanted to check out that she had not caused me 'too much trouble'. I had, at the time, acknowledged that I was stuck and we had worked through a misunderstanding. I was able to say quite truthfully that I had learned something from the situation and was grateful to her for accepting my side of the problem.

Summary

This chapter has been concerned with the ending phase of counselling, with emphasis on preparation for the future. Ways in which changes may be assessed have been suggested, including some which are non-verbal. Particular difficulties which may occur where modifications in behaviour are involved have been outlined and the need to anticipate communicative challenge has been stressed. The alternatives of arranging for review or leaving further contact to the client were discussed in relation to specific communication problems.

The following four chapters (Chapters 7–10) will each focus on one area of communicative impairment, showing the part that psychological intervention currently plays in treatment. A case study focusing on the counselling aspect of work undertaken with the client ends each chapter.

Working with People who Stutter

Views as to the causes of stuttering put forward in the literature over the years range from the psychoanalytic, through maladaptive learning to the neuropsychological. These views influence the ways in which clinicians have approached treatment. At one extreme the dysfluent person is seen as expressing unresolved conflicts in speech behaviour, at the other to be responding to some kind of dis-coordination of function, stemming from an anomaly in the brain. Most practitioners today, however, acknowledge that stuttering is not a unitary disorder. The term is used to describe a range of manifestations of dysfluency, none of which can be assigned to one single causal factor.

Aspects of stuttering

Observed behaviour

Stuttering behaviour can take the form of repetitions of sounds, syllables or words, the prolongation of sounds or a cessation in speech, usually described as a block. All of us manifest such behaviours when uncertain or anxious but for most people who stutter their occurrence is both more marked and more frequent. Around them there is often visible struggle as well as the insertion of extraneous sounds or movements of the face and even limbs. The exception to this is the group of speakers referred to as 'interiorized stutterers', who through changing words or avoiding situations, seldom allow their dysfluency to emerge although they are aware of the possibility most of the time.

The experience from within

People in this group may experience the most severe degree of speech anxiety. Although they may largely succeed in avoiding dysfluency they may 'live in dread' of its occurrence. Friends, work colleagues and even spouses and family may be unaware of any difficulty. Typically they have spoken to no one about it and therefore have not tested out their theory that they would be rejected or at least would fall in others' estimation if the problem was revealed. When someone carries such a secret through many years the sense of being 'a fraud' is added to a deep feeling of inadequacy which may permeate every aspect of their lives.

And there must be few people who stutter who are not in some way troubled by it. Some give the impression that it is simply a frustrating nuisance, while others express intense feelings of being out of control, even panic-stricken, when their speech begins to disintegrate. Those who have been subject to mockery at home or at school, especially where parents and teachers have been impatient or worse, may be deeply angry with the world or feel themselves to be of no account. Even when other children and significant adults have been 'kind', a feeling of being different, of being the object of pity can undermine self-esteem. As we shall see, early intervention, to prevent the development of negative self-concepts is essential.

The development of dysfluency

Dysfluency can develop in many different ways. A young child may begin to repeat syllables and words, at first probably largely unaware of the fact. If something (or someone) draws the child's attention to it he or she may begin to struggle or to tense up and so 'block' on a word which then becomes construed as 'difficult'. Alternatively, the child may pass through this phase and experience no problem. Some children seem to have marked difficulty very early on, often allied to linguistic delay, while others speak fluently for several years before there is any trouble. In the latter instance the parents will often pin-point an event, such as going to a new school or a traumatic experience, which they see as the cause of the onset of stuttering.

Even these few variations suggest that constitutional, environmental and emotional factors may all play a part in the development of stuttering. By the time the person reaches adolescence both his or her own perception of the problem and the ways in which peers and significant adults react to it will have contributed much to the highly individual nature of any particular experience of stuttering. For most practioners there is little doubt that, whatever the original constellation of causal factors, the psychological implications of being dysfluent need to be taken into account when attempting to alleviate the problem.

Approaches to treatment

The speech versus the person
The scope of this chapter allows for only a brief over-view of approaches to the treatment of stuttering (Rustin et al. (1987) is one of many useful sources for further information). Having said that 'most practitioners' would take the psychological implications of being dysfluent into account it should be acknowledged that there *are* those who see no necessity for work on self-concept or attitudinal changes. Their focus is on the refinement of speech techniques and programmes to enable 'normal-sounding' speech to replace dysfluency (e.g. Webster, 1980; Ingham and Onslow, 1985).

For someone who is himself dysfluent, such a view is unacceptable:

> Merely to work with stuttered speech by changing a person's stuttering behaviour through the teaching of a technique, may be viewing the problem too simplistically. To divorce a person's behaviour, to manipulate that behaviour as if it were a set of symptoms, in my opinion curtails and denies access to the factors which perpetuate that behaviour. In short, stuttering cannot exist outwith the person. It would seem necessary to assert that the therapist's approach should accommodate the whole person and his interpretation of the problem. (Insley, 1987: 134)

In practice, clinicians working with people who stutter often employ an approach which combines speech modification procedures and attention to the feelings and perceptions which have developed around the difficulty. At the City Lit, a Centre for stuttering therapy in London, for example, 'block modification therapy' is offered. This involves identification of both the overt and covert aspects of dysfluency; desensitization, in which attitude change is attempted; variation, where experiments with changes both in speech and life-style are undertaken, and finally, modification itself, which entails learning to 'cancel' a stutter and recover from it, to 'pull out' of a block when it occurs and to use the anticipation of stuttering to change the approach to a feared word. (Although this approach is designed for work with groups it can easily be used in individual therapy.) Cooper's Personalized Fluency Control Therapy (1987) is another example of such a combined programme.

Dysfluent children in the family context
With very young children, intervention is usually confined to counselling work with parents. The focus is on their reactions to the child's dysfluency and on means for modifying the environment

in order to prevent disruption and enhance the experience of communication. Tensions within the family are explored for their possible effects on the child and measures taken to ease them. Reference was made in Chapter 1 to the work with families described by Rustin (1987) and Hayhow and Levy (1989). Clifford and Watson (1987) take an Adlerian approach. This involves clarifying with the whole family the child's goals when stuttering, which they classify under the headings of 'four mistaken goals of misbehaviour' – 'attention', 'power', 'revenge' and 'complete inadequacy'. The parents are then asked to change their responses to their child's speech and any disturbing behaviour: to ignore it where attention is sought, to withdraw from any power struggle, not to retaliate when revenge is the goal and to encourage without pampering if the child shows feelings of inadequacy. I personally find the concept of stuttering as 'misbehaviour' disturbing.

In Britain at least adolescents who stutter are traditionally worked with in groups. It is felt that they respond better in the company of peers. The scope for role-play, testing out new ways of approaching social situations and experiencing the pressures of holding their own with a number of people is an obvious advantage. Where a young person is in considerable psychological difficulty, however, their emotional needs are probably best served in a one-to-one situation.

Stuttering as a 'role' problem

Where an Adlerian approach focuses on the person's life goal, others see stuttering as a role which may dominate his or her life. Sheehan (1975) was first to focus powerfully on stuttering as related to the person's perception of self. To him, it is a 'false-role disorder', whereby the person is seen as continually struggling to conceal a behaviour of which he or she is deeply ashamed. Only by accepting the problem and openly acknowledging it to others will the person be free, he maintains, to develop more relaxed and effective communication. Fransella (1972), on the other hand, whose work we discussed in Chapter 2, places emphasis on the need for the person to elaborate a role as a fluent speaker. She found in her research that dysfluent people had highly elaborated networks of ideas about themselves as stutterers, being able to predict how they would behave in a situation, how other people would react to them, but very little knowledge of how things would be if they were fluent. She sees the aim of treatment, therefore, as 'increasing the meaningfulness of being fluent'.

My own work, not only with people who stutter but with those who have eating disorders, leads me to take the issue of self-perception further. It is indeed important for the person to anticipate the implications of change from stuttering to fluency or from overeating to eating normally, but it is also essential to extend self-perception beyond those single bipolar dimensions. Focusing on speaking or eating alone can intensify the preoccupation with the problem and maintain the pendulum swing from one extreme to the other. If the self-view is dilated to embrace what *else* the person is besides a speaker or an eater such preoccupation is diffused and other aspects of their being given enhanced meaning and value.

Special issues in counselling people who stutter

Although it will be clear that approaching dysfluency at the level of speech behaviour alone is felt by many to be inappropriate, it is also acknowledged that some kind of speech modification and attention to communication skills may form an important part of our work with someone who stutters. In this section, however, the focus will be on important issues for the counselling aspect of sessions with older people or those responsible for dysfluent children.

Prevention
When working with the families of young children much is quite rightly made of the need to explore reactions to dysfluency, disruptive factors in the environment and underlying family stresses. Even more important, however, is the question of what might be done to prevent the development of negative self-concepts in the child. The counsellor can help the parents to consider the ways in which, by their behaviour towards the child as well as the things they say, they are defining him or her in limited ways, such as, 'a worrier' or 'shy' or 'not coping'. They need to look for areas of activity where the child seems absorbed and confident and affirm that they are of real importance and part of the child's identity. Often very caring parents are not used to looking at things from the child's point of view and fail to understand why something which to them is of no account has great meaning for the child. A child who is respected in this way by others will have feelings of self-worth and be more able to cope with difficulties without feeling diminished.

Growing awareness of self
By adolescence young people with poor self-esteem may have either retreated into non-communication or have tried to brazen it out

with their fellows. If they are dysfluent they may be teased or simply not listened to and friendships with their own and the opposite sex can be difficult to establish. Many adults who stutter describe this as a time when speech really 'mattered', when issues of success and failure in relationships, in abilities of all kinds began to cluster around their dysfluency. Situations were anticipated largely in terms of the speaking involved and awareness of stuttering became the expectation that they would stutter. Anxiety had become chronic for some. The counsellor needs at this stage to gauge where the young people are in relation to preoccupation with speech.

Where fears for their own performance emerge as predominant the aim will be to loosen habitual approaches to 'difficult' situations with all their resources, not just their speech in mind. Role-play involving meeting new people, for example, can provide opportunities both for changing the focus from self-consciousness to awareness of others and for feedback on the effect that those changes have on the counsellor. If their one mission in life has been to hide their stuttering, learning to refer to it openly can clear the way for them just to 'be' with others. It may be crucial to unravel feelings of guilt or shame about stuttering or anger towards their parents, which can be carried throughout their lives. Most important of all, the young people may need to elaborate their self-concepts to include the many things they are besides stutterers – friends, students, football-players, dancers, humorists, etc. Getting nowhere in my attempt to address this aspect through mere discussion with a 14-year-old boy, I encouraged him to take part in a Venture Holiday. Here he got in touch with resources in himself he did not know he had and thereafter the 'talk' had real meaning for him.

Stuttering in adult life

Although I have said that for many adults too there is a need to dilate the view of self beyond issues of stuttering and fluency, many dysfluent adults have been able to develop a sense of themselves which is far wider in focus than that of 'me the stutterer'. Their work and adult relationships have given them the confidence they lacked as teenagers. Nevertheless, even where they have become effective communicators, the experience of stuttering can still remain a force in their lives. It can become the dumping ground for all that has gone wrong. It can 'explain' failures in relationship and career and prevent their looking more fully at other areas of their functioning which have become 'stuck'. One of the counsellor's main tasks may be to help them to focus more on the feelings they convey and their stance towards others which are having a more negative effect on their marriage, say, or progress at work than any instances of speech failure.

They may have even tighter predictions about certain situations or certain people than adolescents as they have gone unchallenged for longer. They too will need to approach events more fully. Where they continue to project old fears onto people who represent key figures in their lives they will continue to feel inadequate and angry in their presence. Work needs to be done on differentiating the old from the current and learning to read people for what they are. I have described elsewhere (Dalton, 1983, 1987), ways of 'reconstruing' such events and such people.

None of this is to suggest that in counselling dysfluent people of any age the stuttering should be ignored or marginalized. It is only to say that, as with any problem, dysfluency needs to be seen in the context of the whole person, its meaning to him or her clarified and resources brought to bear to reduce its limiting and sometimes immobilizing effects.

An experience of counselling with Matthew

The person

Matthew was a 30-year-old musician, who spent much of his time touring in Britain and abroad. This is what he wrote about himself in his self-characterization (a character sketch of himself, written in the third person as if through the eyes of a sympathetic friend):

> Matthew's shy disposition shows itself in a 'stutter', which hides his better qualities. Since a small boy he has moved house no less than twenty times and lived in many different towns and countries. This has made him able to adapt very quickly to different environments and different people, but at the same time he remains essentially an outsider.
>
> He is apt to take everybody for what they appear to be, almost on first impression, partly because he is not the type to judge people in any critical way and partly because he doesn't often get to know them well. He is himself transparent to a degree, with neither the talent nor the inclination to deceive anybody.
>
> He enjoys and needs the company of others, not necessarily in large numbers (most parties overwhelm him) but just simply to be among other people; he enjoys making himself useful to others and actually enjoys helping people out when they can use him, be it moving house or just washing a pile of dishes!
>
> Matthew is a musician and in fact is quite jealous of his talents, and in his teens and early twenties was quite ambitious, and even now is inspired to practise alone for long periods, aiming for the impossible. This leaves him feeling cut off from the world and makes contact with people even more difficult.

He is a passionate and often strong-willed person underneath his harmless exterior, but he daren't offend anybody directly. As a musician, when he is on form, there is a forcefulness in his playing which briefly transforms him into a confident, fearless being and he can be quite a showman on stage.

With close friends he can show the kind of humour that is sheer ridiculousness and absurdity, something which was part of the language of all his brothers and sisters when they were young, but which he feels is beyond his ability to carry off among his peers now.

(See below for an analysis of this self-characterization.)

The presenting problem

From the outside Matthew's dysfluency appeared mild, but I was aware of considerable tension and of him changing words quite frequently during our first meeting, thus avoiding stuttering. His parents had ignored it and he had felt unable to talk to anyone about it. He had not sought help before this. Recently, however, on reaching his thirtieth year he had 'taken stock' and decided that 'music, although very important, wasn't everything', and that his anxiety about speech was holding him back socially and in relationships with women in particular. He was not seeking a magic cure, only wanted to conquer the fear.

The initial contract

As Matthew could only be sure of remaining in London for the next two months we agreed to eight sessions initially, during which we would explore the problem in the context of his life as a whole, focus on those areas which seemed most relevant and hopefully set change in motion. Depending on how useful he found this approach we would probably continue to work together in blocks of time between tours.

Exploration

During the first few sessions Matthew told his story, described the effects his stutter had on his life and produced the self-characterization.

Analysis of self-characterization

The main themes I noted from Matthew's writing were the immediate reference to his stutter and the link with his shyness, which 'hides his better qualities'. This notion of not showing himself as he truly is is picked up later in the reference to the passionate and strong-willed person underneath the harmless exterior, but seems to be contradicted by his saying that he is 'transparent to a degree'. His sense of being 'an outsider' is linked also with the constant moves throughout his life. His need to be among people, his endeavours to please them and fear of offending them suggest a quite deep lack of social confidence, as does his inability now to show his humour. The 'showman' that he can be as a musician suggests a polarization of himself in different contexts.

Overall my impression was of someone who defined himself largely through a single net-work of constructs around shyness and lack of confidence, with the polar opposites only expressed in his role as a musician.

The story

One key issue relating to his childhood seemed to be the 'conspiracy of silence' surrounding his dysfluency. His father was rather dismissive of him generally, preferring his more extrovert brothers and sisters. He had not approved of his becoming a musician but expressed a grudging pride when he began to do well. His mother, on the other hand, though saying nothing, had always seemed tense and anxious when he stuttered. He felt that she had been overprotective of him as the shy one in the family and she was the only one to whom he could talk about music.

At his many schools he largely got by through keeping quiet. The other children, whom he seldom had time to get to know, left him alone and only one teacher at a primary school, whom he described as a sadist, used Matthew's stutter as a focus of ridicule. He had surprised everyone by his determination to be a musician and gained some confidence in himself as he progressed at college and began to succeed as a professional. He felt now, however, that he wanted to develop his career in a way which would keep him more stably based in London. There were opportunities for teaching which he felt he could do if he were less concerned about speech.

He understood that his itinerant life as well as his reticence contributed to his lack of close friends. His relationships with women seemed to fall into a pattern of being 'taken up' by rather motherly women of all ages, from whom he fairly soon ran a mile, feeling suffocated. He had been attracted to one or two others, who were more 'lively' and 'humorous' but had not had the courage to approach them. When I asked him how he thought various people saw him he had very little idea, beyond his mother's view of him as 'reserved, sensitive and kind' and his father's as 'introverted, a first-class musician and a bit of a mystery'. He took it for granted that those who realized that he stuttered thought him 'timid' and 'weak'.

Initial aims

Given more time at this stage I would have liked to go more deeply with him into his relationships with his family, but it seemed important to focus on the here and now. His preoccupation with hiding his dysfluency was the most immobilizing factor in his perception of himself and in his ways of relating to others. A fluency technique, therefore, was likely, at this stage at least, to lock him still further into the limiting patterns he had established. We agreed on the following immediate goals:

1   To begin to tackle avoidance by saying everything he wanted to say without changing words in these sessions.
2   To test out his theory that revealing his dysfluency would have a negative effect on others. (He was quite fearful of this, but recognized that trying to hide it had distanced him from people. It also threw into question the notion expressed in his writing that he had 'neither the talent nor the inclination to deceive anybody'.)
3   To focus on others when in a group in order to construe them more fully and discriminatively. (Currently he seemed to see them largely in terms of shyness or extroversion.)
4   To take up an offer of a few sessions of teaching in order to see whether his confidence in his skills could override his speech anxiety.

The experiments

With experiment 1, although at first Matthew blocked more frequently during the sessions his speech was, on the whole, less disjointed. He found it difficult for a while not to apologize, but began to believe that I was more interested in *what* he said than *how* he said it.

For experiment 2, Matthew chose two people to begin with to whom he would speak about his stutter. The first was his neighbour, whom he had known for some years and with whom he occasionally had coffee. He invited him in during the following week and during the course of conversation mentioned his dysfluency. The man had not noticed, showed only mild interest and immediately went on to ask about his latest tour of

France. This in itself helped put things in perspective. He had assumed that stuttering was as important to others as it was to himself.

The second person was the colleague whose sessions of teaching he had been offered. He *had* noticed Matthew's stuttering on occasions but as he had no trouble when they were discussing how they would interpret the music they were playing together, it had not occurred to him that he would have any difficulty teaching. This led us to explore more fully the circumstances in which Matthew was fluent. When he was 'being a musician' he seldom thought about speech and rarely had difficulty. When he was 'being social' he was self-conscious, speech-conscious and in trouble.

I asked him to try to clarify other differences in himself besides his speech in these two contrasting situations. He felt that in the former he was 'more assertive', 'more in touch with others' and 'funnier'! This added meaning to experiment number 3, where he was to focus more on others and to be more in touch with them. To begin with I suggested that he make no particular effort to speak more (and perhaps not to crack jokes just yet) but concentrate on listening and taking in the situation as a whole, the people around him and what he understood about how they were feeling and seeing things.

The results of a number of these experiences proved very useful. It took time for him to free himself from self-consciousness but removing the pressure to contribute, which he had always felt, helped him to sit back and relax. He acknowledged that he was able to take in far more of what others were saying and to 'weigh them up' more clearly. When he described them to me he produced a much wider range of attributions than the 'shy/ extrovert' dimension. Once or twice he found himself joining in spontaneously, without the anticipatory fear. There was a long way to go here, but it was a useful beginning.

With experiment 4, his colleague's faith in him as a teacher gave him courage to try and he came in quite triumphantly to a session saying that he had 'killed two birds with one stone'. Faced with a group of students he felt the familiar dryness in his mouth and tightening of his chest. However, he looked at each of them in turn and then, to his own astonishment, said 'I'm Matthew and, among other things, I stutter. So have a bloody good laugh now and we can get on.' The students duly laughed, Matthew picked up his instrument and began to play. He was in his role as a musician. The fact that he stuttered a few times, he said, did not seem to matter.

Review of the initial phase

During our last agreed session, before Matthew was to go off on tour we reviewed what had occurred so far. Although he seldom avoided words with me and had been able to mention his dysfluency to a few people, he still tried to hide it in some situations. When 'being a musician' he could consistently be both more fluent and less concerned when he did stutter. Learning to listen and turn the focus from himself onto others had helped him when 'being social' but the role was still too tightly enmeshed with old fears and too undifferentiated. And he still felt 'like a gauche schoolboy' in the presence of most women. The teaching had gone well and he was actively seeking more long-term work at one of the colleges in London.

Matthew had no doubt that he was going in the right direction and wanted to go on with counselling when he returned to London in two months' time. He agreed to continue working on his construing of other people and to be more open about his stuttering where it was not too threatening. In addition, I asked him to keep a diary during the break with the focus on elaborating roles other than that of musician and the undifferentiated social self. He was due to visit his parents while on tour and was to take particular note of how he was with each of them and see if he could learn more about them. Before he left he was determined, for the first time, to speak to them about his stutter.

Phase 2

When Matthew returned in the autumn he had a good deal to report. The tour had gone well and he had enjoyed the social aspect of it more than usual. He had met a young woman musician at one stage and felt that he had made the beginnings of a relationship with her. He told her about his difficulty with an ease that surprised him and had not felt diminished by this. The most important event, however, had been his visit to his parents, which he described as illuminating.

He felt that he had been able to stand back and be much more aware of what was going on between himself and them. With his father he encountered the expected, slightly embarrassed, bluff humour. His father had enquired about 'the music' and expressed pleasure at how things were going. Uncharacteristically, Matthew had to admit, he asked his father how his business was going and learned for the first time of his considerable anxiety about it. It had not occurred to him that he was anything but confident and highly successful. When he spoke to him about his stutter he learned that his father was very concerned when he was young but had been told (by a speech therapist!) to ignore it. When Matthew had become more able to hide the dysfluency he assumed that it was no longer a problem.

It had always puzzled Matthew that, although he felt at ease with his mother, he was more dysfluent with her than almost anyone. During his visit this time he understood why. He noticed that every time he spoke she would look at him with particular attention, her head slightly to one side and a rather anxious smile on her face. She was, in fact, waiting for him to stutter. He felt quite angry with her, confronted her with what she was doing and demanded why she had never encouraged him to talk about his speech with her. She too protested that she had been told to ignore it. He came away feeling less in awe of his father and more sympathetic towards him. But he was clearly beginning to question his mother's role in his life.

Renewed aims

It seemed likely at this stage that Matthew would be in or around London for several months and able to come for a session most weeks. He had a number of concerts and some commitments as a relief teacher at a college where he hoped to be employed on a more permanent basis. I suggested the following aims:

1   To generalize the elimination of word-avoidance and to acknowledge his dysfluency by systematically widening the range of people with whom he was prepared to be open.
2   To elaborate other roles besides that of musician, which he now referred to as 'the performer' and the undifferentiated social self, 'the mouse'. (He had begun to make some sketchy notes in his diary.)
3   To explore further the relationships with members of his family in order to see what effects they might have on relationships outside it.

Further experiments

As a result of experiment 1 in the second phase, the most striking effect of Matthew gradually becoming more open about his dysfluency was the relief he experienced from reduced anxiety. He had felt unacceptable when a 'secret stutterer' but found himself accepted when he acknowledged the difficulty. Very few people understood the seriousness of its meaning to him and only when I asked him to try to put himself in the shoes of someone with a hearing loss, perhaps, or some other disability did he realize how little we all understand about the personal experience of particular difficulties. He gradually found himself able to take his part in most conversations, only falling silent when overwhelmed by the more articulate and ebullient of his colleagues.

Such involvement with others allowed him to experience a wider range of ways of being than the performer and the mouse (second phase, experiment 2). When I got him to describe his encounters with people he was clearly responding to them in more differentiated ways. As 'a friend' he could be 'serious and thoughtful' or 'jokey'. Although still liking to please others he became more assertive and more able to ask things of them. He also began to elaborate his role as 'a teacher', which he enjoyed, finding that he could be both facilitating and challenging. As the sessions went on he referred less and less to his speech and more to his music, his teaching and his expanding social life.

Throughout the second phase sessions we were also looking at his relationships with his parents and two of his brothers in particular (experiment 3). The visit to his home had caused him to challenge a number of assumptions about his father. Until he had moved from his concern with himself and the impression his father had of him to ask him how things were with him, he had no idea that he too could be anxious and unsure. He had taken it for granted that his father's air of 'rightness' and control and his doubts about music as a 'man's job' meant that he was both a Philistine and supremely confident of his place in the world. But Matthew began to wonder whether he too would have liked to do something he enjoyed, rather than feel obliged to make money to provide for his large family.

The anger he had experienced towards his mother on that visit confused him. He had realized that she had been overprotective but was now inclined to blame her for being so passive about his speech problem, even making it worse through her unspoken anxiety. It seemed to me that here he was experiencing feelings that belonged to an earlier time, to his adolescence, when he might himself have made moves to free himself from his dependence on her. We set up a role-play situation, where first he spoke to me, as his mother, in the way that he had done when he last saw her. I felt that he was looking to me for encouragement and almost demanding sympathy. Then I suggested he spoke to her as he did to me, in an adult way, and told her some of the new things in his life that we talked about. He was aware of the difference and realized that whatever communication he had with his mother was governed as much by what he brought to her as her attitude towards him.

When he first began to say more about his siblings he described them and their effects on him very much as a 'group'. They were lively, noisy, articulate and busy. Then I asked him to write a sketch of each of them in turn. From this his two elder brothers emerged as especially significant. Charles was a successful academic, quick-witted and sarcastic, who liked to put Matthew down. He seemed to be the prototype for people he met now whom he found difficult to keep up with. The question was, did he need to try to keep up with them? Could he just 'let them get on with it'? Robert was less bright but full of energy, very physical and, of all the family, the one whose high spirits swamped any company he was in. He made Matthew feel dull and uninteresting, just as the more 'dynamic' members of orchestras did now. But, was this contrasting picture of himself the only one?

On reflection he felt that he could begin to see himself and his siblings as a family of different individuals, each one distinct in his or her own way. There was no need to weigh himself against them and find himself the 'weak' one or the 'shy' one. As he was now less isolated from those he worked with it was possible to challenge current negative self-comparisons too. These had undoubtedly influenced his expectations of relating easily to women and here too there was promise of change.

Review of phase 2

This second phase consisted of twelve sessions, with one or two short breaks over a period of four months. Although he occasionally substituted words and avoided speaking, this was now rare and his anxiety had decreased greatly. Still quiet in a large group of people he did not feel diminished by this and expressed himself content to be an onlooker sometimes. Prospects for developing his teaching were good and thus his aim to feel more grounded in one place likely to be fulfilled.

I was not sure how far his reflections on his relationship with his mother was leading to change or what effect it might have on his ways of relating to other women. I considered encouraging him to go more deeply into this area, but decided against it as he had not shown any inclination to address issues of his sexuality which I felt might be involved here. Rightly or wrongly, while 'making space' for further exploration, as a counsellor I never introduce new material unless I feel invited to do so by something a client says or does. It seemed probable, too, that his perception of himself as a whole would need to elaborate more fully over time and I hoped that we had done enough to set this in train.

Having reviewed what had been accomplished, we agreed to end the series. He knew that he could contact me in the future if he wished, but seemed hopeful that he would continue to move on.

Summary

This chapter has focused on stuttering, one of the major areas of communication difficulty addressed in this book. Some of the main approaches to treatment have been discussed, together with special issues involved in working with dysfluent children, young people and adults. The case study of 'Matthew' develops many of these themes more fully.

In Chapter 8 counselling in relation to voice disorders is the topic. As with dysfluency, the work here can also involve direct behaviour modification work but the emphasis will be on the causes and effects of psychogenic voice problems.

8

Counselling and Vocal Rehabilitation

In Chapter 7 stuttering was presented as a concept which covers a wide range of disorders of fluency, each resulting from a number of causal factors. Similarly, dysphonia refers to voice problems whose bases may lie in organic pathology, such as a congenital abnormality, endocrine disorder, tumour, trauma, neurological disease or infection, or be psychological in origin, relating to social, interpersonal and intrapersonal stress. This distinction, however, does not in itself indicate that non-psychological intervention only is appropriate for the former and psychological intervention for the latter. The experience of dysphonia of whatever origin can cause considerable stress and a vocal mechanism which is misused due to anxiety or unexpressed conflict may itself show physical signs of damage.

Voice and communication

Many aspects of non-verbal communication influence our construing of other people. The voice is one of the most powerful factors in our initial impressions of another. If it is loud and harsh we are generally put off, unless the context demands it, as perhaps at a political rally. A whining voice suggests complaint and self-pity and does not inspire confidence. A 'silky' voice will persuade some and inspire deep mistrust in others. How far normal voice quality expresses the person within and how far it is 'accidental' is hard to say. A physical defect can certainly give an entirely erroneous impression. Sharp changes caused by infection or misuse can make people seem quite unlike themselves. And there is little doubt that we are affected by the sound we hear.

In the absence of factors limiting the use of voice, most people have a wide range of vocal expression which can convey meaning and emotion: 'If we feel liberated and vibrant our voices sound open and energetic. If we feel hurried and impatient, our voices sound quick and sharp. If we are convulsed by sobbing, our voices are broken and uncontrolled' (Butcher et al., 1993: 1). Quite small changes in the voice of someone we know well can signal particular moods or attitudes which may contradict the words spoken. In the counselling situation, facial and bodily tensions may alert us to a degree of anxiety not expressed by a deceptively calm voice. The sound we hear, therefore, should be construed in the context of the total communication.

Audible characteristics of dysphonia

Aronson (1990: 6) says that a voice disorder exists 'when quality, pitch, loudness or flexibility differs from the voices of others of similar age, sex and cultural group'. Dysphonic voice quality may be described variously as hoarse, husky, creaky, breathy, hyper-nasal and hyponasal. The pitch will obviously be judged as inappropriate if a young man, say, continues to produce a child's voice or a woman the deep throaty tones of a bass-baritone. Excessive loudness may be socially unacceptable, but is not usually classed as disordered unless vocal strain accompanies it. A very soft voice, however, can manifest weakness of the respiratory or laryngeal musculature or express the speaker's reluctance to be heard. A voice without flexibility or lacking varied intonation may again be the result of neurological impairment or express the flatness felt by someone who is depressed. Total loss of voice, or aphonia, can be caused by a range of organic factors or occur psychologically, due to shock or a longer-term retreat into silence under stress.

Personal perception

Most people are taken by surprise the first time they hear their own voices on tape. The words and the meaning are theirs but the voice sounds alien. This is in part due to the fact that we hear our own voices from within our skulls, through bone-conduction of sound, while for others it is transmitted through air waves. It is not surprising, then, that external judgements of the voice will differ from the person's own perception. When something goes wrong, others may say that a woman sounds 'sexy', for example, while she herself is conscious of constriction and discomfort. The quality may be quite disturbing to listen to, without the person's realizing it. Being unable to project the voice in order to be heard in normal conversation can be deeply frustrating and if the situation goes on for any length of time we begin to feel alienated. The experience of even temporary aphonia has been described in terms of isolation, a turning inwards on oneself. Loss of voice due to laryngectomy is loss of part of the self which cannot be restored.

Approaches to treatment

The scope of this chapter allows for only a brief look at the non-psychological aspects of treatment for dysphonia. Details of approaches to the management of the full range of voice problems can be found in M. Fawcus (1991) and Greene and Mathieson (1989).

Physical aspects
Treatment for dysphonia in the speech and language therapy setting is always preceded by careful assessment. In the context of the person's history and medical information from the ENT (ear, nose and throat) department as to the functioning and state of the vocal chords, a voice evaluation will cover general and specific physical tension, respiration, pitch of voice, loudness and resonance. According to this assessment, a period of voice rest, work on relaxation, breathing technique, the establishment of optimum pitch and the development of appropriate resonance will be among those areas of the physical work undertaken. Even where the problem is diagnosed as psychogenic in origin, some of these physical procedures will be employed. Anxiety, for example, often manifests itself in excessive tension, disruption of breathing and persistent use of inappropriate pitch and loudness. These, as has been said, can themselves result in vocal abuse.

Environmental aspects
Careful note is always taken of any environmental factors which may be contributing to a voice problem. If the person smokes or works or lives in a polluted atmosphere, measures need to be taken to reduce exposure to such harm. Having to make oneself heard amid constant noise may be exacerbating the problem. Extensive use of voice in itself should not alone cause dysphonia. But where there is misuse, through forcing or inappropriate pitch, these too must receive attention.

Psychological aspects
Included in any evaluation of dysphonia will be reference to chronic or current causes of psychological stress, be they inter-personal or related to a troubled sense of self. Anxiety may be found to play its part in problems showing organic effects, such as vocal nodules and contact ulcers, where excessive musculoskeletal tension is involved. Children with chronic hoarseness or recurrent voice loss are often hyperactive and aggressive. It may be important to explore with them their problems with life, family

tensions, relationships with peers and teachers, before we can hope to help them to relax and develop more appropriate vocal habits. Hodkinson (1991) believes that it is vital for parents to be involved in ongoing counselling where children are found to be at risk of chronic vocal problems.

Reference was made in Chapter 1 to the need to address issues of self-perception in boys with mutational voice disorders and explore with them the meaning of voice change, alongside any attempts to elicit a lower register. R. Fawcus (1991: 305) includes a number of psychological elements which might need to be addressed in his list of causes of puberphonia: 'a desire to retain a successful soprano voice that has brought distinction . . . fear of assuming a full share of adult responsibility' among them. But he also regards the initial rejection of a new, deeper voice by many clients as understandable and says that appropriate 'advice and counselling can usually overcome this very human, quite normal reaction to change' (1991: 309), which he likens to the fear which may be experienced with the sudden acquisition of fluency.

Butcher et al. (1993: 10) found from the literature and their own research that voice disorders diagnosed as psychogenic in adults were commonly associated with acute or long-term anxiety, difficulty in expressing feelings, particularly anger, and 'over-commitment and helplessness'. These authors make a distinction between this group and people with 'conversion disorders', where function is impaired in the absence of organic signs: 'Symptoms commonly appear during periods of stress and can serve the function of helping the sufferer avoid decision, responsibility, action or relationship difficulties' (1993: 7). They see the conditions as rare and, like other so-called 'hysterical' disorders, usually intractable to many forms of psychological help.

One area where speech and language therapists may find themselves involved is that of transsexualism. Here, clearly, the clients' psychological needs go far beyond the issue of a change in voice. They go through quite stringent psychological assessment to ensure that the choice they make to change their sex has been fully explored and may be referred for psychotherapy by their consultant psychiatrist. But as Challoner (1991: 237) points out, it is often the speech and language therapist, working with them on their voice, who provides the main opportunity for reflecting on their feelings about being 'the wrong gender' all their lives and for looking at the implications of so major a change. Therapists involved in such work often have had counselling training but, she believes, 'each must recognize the limits of his or her expertise' and 'techniques used should be largely based on listening and helping the client to reflect back on what he has said'.

Current psychological approaches

A survey of speech and language therapists in the UK (Elias et al., 1989) revealed that counselling, behaviour therapy, personal construct therapy, psychotherapy and hypnosis formed part of the rehabilitation programme for psychogenic voice disorders in many clinical settings. Anxiety control training, as developed by Snaith (1981), is also frequently employed. Unfortunately, detailed accounts of these approaches to voice are rare. One notable exception can be found in Butcher et al. (1993). Here, a cognitive–behaviour therapy model is presented, assessment procedures discussed and aspects of treatment illustrated, with a number of very useful case studies.

They summarize their approach thus:

> The main areas of focus in assessment are on understanding the relationship between environmental life events, personal relationships, thoughts and images and emotional, physiological and behavioural reactions. Particular stress is, however, put on the way that emotional disturbance and associated difficulties are created or exacerbated by errors in thinking and problem solving.

They go on to say that therapy

> emphasizes establishing a sound therapeutic relationship, demystification, collaboration, self-help, active data collection, altering irrational or negative beliefs, self-instruction, cognitive and behavioural target setting and multiple treatment strategies. (Butcher et al., 1993: 51)

Although, as the survey referred to above found, a personal construct approach to vocal rehabilitation is being taken by speech and language therapists, as yet nothing has appeared in the literature. Having some similarities to a cognitive behavioural approach, there are differences of emphases. PCP assessment or exploration does not prescribe the areas to be investigated, rather leaving it to the clients, through the elicitation of their construing and elaboration through laddering and other procedures, self-characterizations and grids, to indicate what is important to them. Their theories about themselves and others are tested for their effectiveness in the context of their current experience. Where someone has seen 'keeping quiet' as the only alternative to confrontation in the face of bullying, for example, he or she may transfer resources from other ways of relating to the situation which is found to be intolerable.

An experience of counselling with Jade

The person

Jade was a lively, attractive woman in her early forties, who came for an initial meeting, referred by a colleague who had worked with her on ways of relaxing and preserving her voice for a few sessions. She was under considerable stress at work in a commercial film company and wanted to find ways of dealing with that situation in particular and her tendancy to 'overreact and end up the fall-guy' in general. She had done well professionally over the years describing herself as 'a good organizer' rather than 'an ideas person'. She lived alone but had a number of close friends and was ambivalent about the issue of having a stable partner. She had had several quite long-standing relationships with men, which she thought it would be useful to explore. She loved having fun, eating and drinking, but, more than anything, 'conversation'.

The presenting problem

Jade's voice was quite hoarse and she had to remind herself not to force it. It had been giving her trouble off and on for about two years and she could lose it completely when she was severely stressed. ENT investigation had found nothing to suggest a cause and she seemed to accept the reassurance that 'there was nothing sinister'. She was convinced herself that her hoarseness expressed her tension and frustration. She could not get through to her boss at work and it was as if she sometimes just gave up trying by losing her voice.

The initial contract

Although Jade was concerned that her voice should improve she said she felt that it was about time she addressed a number of issues to do with her feelings about herself and some of her relationships, past and present. Although not clear how, she believed them to be linked with her dysphonia. I explained something of the PCP approach and she agreed to four exploratory sessions, during which she wanted to look at aspects of her childhood to see how they affected her ways of dealing with things now. After that it should be clear whether the approach was what she was looking for and we should have some idea of what a counselling series would entail. I asked her to write a self-characterization, which she posted to me before we met again.

Exploration

Jade had spent much of our first meeting talking about her mother, who had died some six years previously. The picture as she spoke was of her mother's instability and her own feeling from an early age that she had to look after her. The self characterization was an elaboration of this theme, covering her life from birth until early childhood. She described her mother as 'not strong emotionally', 'pretty and vivacious' and 'something of a flirt'. She had had a nervous breakdown after the birth of her son and become 'paralysed' for several months. Jade's earliest memories were of rocking her brother to sleep and bathing her mother's legs with oil.

The feeling of tension and turmoil in the writing is very strong – for example, mother quarrelling with her sister who lived with them, the violence of several men who were her lovers. Jade saw herself as spending those early years in fear and insecurity. She herself became afflicted with a mysterious skin disease which prevented her from opening her eyes after her mother had said that she would have the children looked after so that she could work. It was possible that this early somatization of distress, also shown by her mother, was reoccuring now in her dysphonia.

When we looked at the self-characterization together Jade became quite tearful, at first saying that it 'hurt' to cry, then that it was trying *not* to cry that hurt. She always knew that her mother loved her but had felt that she could never 'measure up' to what was expected of her. Although her mother depended on her more and more as time went on she criticized Jade continually, for how she looked, for not being 'witty and clever'. At the age of eighteen she left home and although the tensions between herself and her mother eased after this Jade was grieving now that they had not resolved things between them before she died. She wanted both to confront her with the hurt she had caused and tell her how much she loved her.

At the end of the session I suggested to Jade that she write a letter to her mother, saying all that she wanted to say, set it aside and then try to read it as if she were her mother. She asked if she could bring it to me so that I could do the same, to which I agreed. When I read it I found it very moving and felt that Jade had got to the heart of feelings that had troubled her for many years. Although she referred to her often after this I believe the writing contributed to her feeling more at peace with her mother.

During the following session we drew together some of the elements in this relationship which seemed to affect later ones: her fear/expectation of anger from anyone she became close to; her difficulty in dealing with criticism, which always left her diminished; her need to 'look after' people, however they behaved towards her. These themes were found in all of her longer-term relationships with men and brought us to the focus of her current stress at work, her boss.

'Daniel' was the managing director of the film company and Jade, as his senior partner, had a great deal of responsibility for the day-to-day running of things. He was an extremely volatile man, who could explode uncontrollably. Jade was the buffer between him and the others working for the company and between him and their clients. He was at once deeply dependent on her and fiercely critical, blaming her when things went wrong. Although Jade fought him, she felt that she always lost, as he was very articulate and cutting. Recently he had begun to put her down in front of clients, which left her speechless (and voiceless) with rage and frustration. She was not in love with him, but seemed trapped by his need for her.

Jade was far less clear at this stage about her own needs. She recognized that she always took the role of carer. She had two younger sisters from her mother's second marriage, whom she frequently 'bailed out', financially and emotionally, and they were very important to her. She felt loved by them but, although they were both in their thirties, referred to them still as her 'little sisters'. When I asked her how it would feel to be 'looked after' herself, she had to think before she said it would be wonderful for a change. She had a close woman friend, 'Karen' who took care of her dog when she was at work and with whom she talked endlessly about her friend's unhappy marriage and difficult young daughter and her own social and working life. But her giving was not unconditional and she could be critical of the way Jade led her life, leaving her feeling that Karen was in some way a 'better person' than herself.

Areas for change

One striking aspect both of these early conversations and Jade's writing was how much of the time she spent talking about other people, analysing them, describing *herself* only in relation to their effects on her, how she responded to their anger, criticism, loving or dependency. The need for her to establish boundaries between herself and others, to experience herself more as a separate person, would underlie any of the more tangible changes attempted.

During the last of our agreed four sessions I set out what seemed to me to be the areas where Jade could work for change.

1   Finding alternative ways of dealing with anger.
2   Desensitizing herself to criticism and reviewing doubts about her competency.
3   Loosening of intensity/tension through more discriminative reactions to things.

Item 3 was more directly aimed at helping with management of her voice problem. Change in items 1 and 2 should reduce the underlying stress and therefore also affect her use of voice. Changes in self-perception, clearly sought in item 2, were implicit in the other two. The three areas of concern overlapped and we worked on them concurrently during the ensuing twenty or more sessions.

Aspects of change over time

Jade was in something of a crisis over her relationship with Daniel. His irascibility and instability seemed to be increasing and she had had thoughts of leaving the company. However, she had invested much of herself, not to say her capital, in building it up, did not want to let the others down and knew that she would feel 'a failure' if she quit, just as she had done when she left home and ended other relationships after a long struggle.

In this tight connection between such theoretically different relationships there seemed to be no distinction between the personal and the professional. When we explored her feelings for Daniel it seemed clear that she was neither sexually attracted to him nor did she respect him. They had been through much together in starting the enterprise, but she felt that she had earned her stake in it and owed him nothing. Being doubtful of her ability to come across well at formal meetings she was happy to organize presentations for clients and leave the talking and the charm to him. But why had she taken it upon herself to stand between him and the staff, bearing the brunt of his dissatisfaction with them and their angry confusion at his contradictory orders?

Drawing professional boundaries

Changing this situation entailed experiment at two levels. First and most urgently she needed to find ways of dealing with Daniel's behaviour at less cost to herself – to stand back more and not let herself be drawn into his turmoil and to be a separate person in her own right. At the moment, when he erupted, she attempted to defend herself and others by 'blustering', which often ended with her in tears. What were the alternatives? She could simply refuse to be shouted at and remove herself from the scene or she could stand her ground in silence to see whether that brought him to a halt.

She tried the first and found that leaving him to simmer down had at least a short-term effect. The second was much harder for her but, when she had mastered it, she had a far greater feeling of control, which was new to her. Daniel was astonished at the change and deeply uneasy. This led to his inviting her for a drink one evening, hoping, she felt, to win her over. He shared with her his acute anxiety about the recession and his fear of losing everything. Jade expressed sympathy, but kept her distance, told him how she felt about what went on and how she wished their relationship to change. For a while there was a truce.

The second experiment involved breaking her isolation from the rest of the staff so that she did not have to carry aggression from all directions. Jade was concerned not to be disloyal but became more open about her position with one or two senior members, who had understood something of the situation but felt powerless to change anything while she continued to cover up for Daniel. They had been unable to establish an appropriate relationship with her and clarify their own position in the company. Their support as well as her greater detachment from him enabled her to have a far greater sense of her own professional role and to withstand his tantrums when they recurred.

Drawing personal boundaries

As the weeks went by Jade's voice improved, with only occasional days when her throat and chest felt 'tight'. She related these more to fatigue than stress as she led a very active social as well as working life. From time to time in sessions we looked at the ways in which she could conserve her voice and her energy more effectively. She did know how to relax and to speak less forcefully, but found it difficult to maintain the new behaviours when feeling under pressure.

Then she arrived for a session extremely hoarse and clearly distressed. She had spoken of the ups and downs of her relationship with her friend Karen from time to time and now they had had a fierce argument, which lasted deep into the previous night. Jade had met a new man friend for a drink and been late picking up her dog, whom Karen looked after during the day. She found herself arraigned as 'selfish', 'uncaring', 'a fool about men' and much else besides. Jade felt that she had handled it all very badly, been defensive, hurt by the hail of criticism, and regressed to an old familiar feeling of Karen's moral superiority.

It seemed important to unravel Karen's problems from Jade's here. She was unhappy in her marriage and clearly envied Jade for her success in work, her many good friendships and her attractiveness to men. She had always disapproved of Jade's boyfriends and saw herself as proved right when relationships came to an end. On her side, Jade felt that she had been a loyal friend over the years, never 'ditching' her when involved in a relationship and always trying to help her to enhance her rather bleak existence. Where she went wrong, she felt, was in her defensiveness. When she was late she always telephoned Karen to warn her but realized that she never said sorry, simply waited for her disapproval.

Knowing that the two talked about 'everything' together I wondered how much Jade had fanned Karen's envy by endlessly discussing the various men in her life. She acknowledged that she might well have done – and made Karen feel even more invalidated as a woman. Another area where there had always been a lack of understanding between them was Karen's handling of her daughter. According to Jade she allowed the 7-year-old to walk all over her and gave her no guidelines as to how to behave. Here it was Karen's turn to be sensitive to criticism. When we reflected on this it seemed that Karen invested all her unconditional love in the child and longed for that love to be returned. Linking her own experience of caring for people who treated her badly with this situation Jade recognized a vulnerability in Karen which she had not fully understood.

Criticism and self-evaluation
Although one purpose of focusing on this important relationship had been to clarify what belonged to Karen and what Jade needed to own as hers, it brought us once more up against one of Jade's greatest difficulties: her catastrophic reaction to criticism. Its origins were clearly in the relationship with her mother. She was dealing with it better in her work situation. But in personal relationships in the past and now she could be devasted and lose all sense of being the 'OK person' she felt herself to be most of the time.

It proved useful to look at this problem in terms of some of the important constructs she had about herself. When not feeling under fire she saw herself as 'strong and potent' (as opposed to 'weak'), 'coping' (versus 'panicking'), 'socially successful' (versus 'awkward'), 'warm and loving' (versus 'angry and hurtful'). What seemed to occur when challenged by criticism was the experience of a comprehensive shift from the positive to the contrast poles of these and other constructs. Before this process could be prevented it was important to explore the underlying lack of confidence which made her so vulnerable.

It seemed clear that Jade had always made comparisons between herself and those close to her and found that she 'didn't match up'. Her mother had been 'pretty ' and made it clear to Jade that she was not. She and two of her boyfriends shared Daniel's gift of articulateness and, often cruel, wit. Jade could be left floundering in her attempts to keep up with them verbally. Karen had 'strong moral principles', sticking to her indifferent husband and caring for her cantankerous father, while Jade had walked out on relationships and owed no duty to child or parent (the fact that she mothered her two younger sisters was seen as foolishness, rather than caring).

As we went through this list of negative comparisons Jade recognized that much of the criticism she objected to from others came from within herself. I suggested that we look at these and other areas to see if there were ways of defining herself other than by contrast. What were the qualities which brought her her friends? She may not have the prettiness and flirtatiousness which brought a stream of men to her mother's door, but she was clearly attractive in her warmth and caring and had sustained friendships with men and women over many years. Her notion that she was inarticulate I could challenge directly, as we had by now had hours of conversation during which she could express herself with great clarity and intelligence. Although her sexual relationships had all ended there seemed no doubt that she had committed herself to them wholeheartedly.

She did, then, have a sense of herself which allowed her to say 'Yes, I do like me!' How could she maintain this feeling in the face of adverse reactions from others? In fact, the work had already begun. Standing back to look at Daniel and Karen had led her to a better understanding of the axes *they* had to grind. While feeling in some ways even more warmly towards Karen as she understood her vulnerabilities better, Jade was less inclined to assume that she was 'morally right' in all her judgements. Separating herself from the role of Daniel's protector had enabled her to see more clearly the extent of the man's irrationality and lack of any real control. As a professional colleague it was not *her* job to unravel his problems. In fact, she gave him the name of a counsellor, should he ever decide that he wanted help.

She also needed, however, to change her own response to criticism in a fairly deliberate way. She had often spoken of her defensiveness and although the work we had done helped her to feel less attacked, her automatic reaction of fierce verbal self-defence remained. This also linked with her tendency to blurt out responses before she gave herself time to think in situations in which she was unsure of her ground: in company meetings sometimes, as well as discussions with friends. Again, I was able to draw her attention to an alternative which she already practised during our sessions. She could be thoughtful and allow quite long silences when she wanted to reflect. She said that this was because she felt under no threat. I asked her to experiment with behaving 'as if' there were no threat in other situations, to give herself (and others) pause for thought. It took some time to establish this new pattern, but it had the added effect of giving her the space to re-evaluate the reality of 'threat' in a number of contexts.

Loosening intensity

Extreme reactions to events, whether great or small, can trouble many of us. To some people to be 'intense' is the only alternative to being dull and uninteresting. Clients who complain of sharp mood-swings never the less may have a real fear of the flatness they associate with equilibrium. Too much intensity can, however, be exhausting for the person concerned and difficult for others to handle. Where there is a communication problem, such as dysfluency or dysphonia, extreme emotionality can exacerbate the problem. The person who stutters cannot hope to speak with ease and someone with a voice problem will inevitably put pressure on breathing and vocalization.

How, then, to help someone to be less reactive without loss of spontaneity? This issue had run through the sessions with Jade. In some areas she had made real progress: with anger, verbal defensiveness, being caught up in another's emotionality. But still, when she spoke of events, she often became very intense and her voice grew louder and more forced. She loved to talk and the image I had of her meetings with friends suggested non-stop excited conversation for hours on end. She could, as I said, be thoughtful and reflective. It was a genuine part of her. She could be good listener. At what point did it all run away with her?

During one session she was telling me of some difficulty her younger sister was in and I noticed a change in her expression. Her voice grew louder and her body more tense. I stopped her and asked her if she had felt the change. With some difficulty she was able to clarify the experience. When she had started to speak she said she was 'describing' what was going on, it was as if she could see it in her mind. Then she was 'living' it, feeling her sister's distress and frustration. I asked her to go on and try to 'describe', to picture as she had done at first. She was able to do this and her voice was normal. The process seemed to entail some kind of inner movement from being totally caught up in the centre of what she was telling to stepping back to visualize it from outside. She was now clear about the difference of the experience and aimed to try to be aware of it over the next few days.

This was far, of course, from resulting in calm detachment at all times. But it served to alert Jade to increases in intensity and gave her the choice of stepping back. She had tried to decrease the rate of her speech, the loudness of her voice with little long-lasting success. This more inward modification seemed more promising. She also found that she could pull herself out of sudden emotional responses to things if she had an internal image of stepping back. One example came when a client was rude to her at a meeting. Her immediate wish was to shout back, but she left a silence instead which was far more powerful than anything she could have said.

Coming to an end

Jade had been coming once a fortnight, then once every three weeks for some time and we began to look towards ending the series. We had, as we went along, reflected on change processes as they occurred and one useful way of summarizing change, particularly in self-perception, which had been central to the work we had been doing, would be to set up a rated grid. This could include the elements 'Me now', 'Me 18 months ago', when she first came for therapy, and 'Me as I would like to be in the future'. Jade liked the idea and I prepared a grid for her using constructs from her writing, some which had recurred through the sessions and a few which I elicited at this time. Figure 8.1 sets out the constructs and elements together with her ratings.

Scanning the ratings of the three 'Self' elements it is clear that on most constructs Jade sees herself as having made some change in the right direction and wishes, on the whole, to go still further. One exception is construct 3, 'sensitive to criticism' versus 'can cope with criticism'. Here she rates herself as very sensitive eighteen months ago, only slightly less so now and wishes to be able to cope very much better in the future. Construct 7 also shows a desire for greater change – she is rather less intense than

#	Left pole	Lena	Martin	Grandmother	Me as I'd like to be in the future	Derek	Ivan	Ron	Me now	Alex	Andrew	Mary	Sarah	Eileen	Me 18 months ago	Karen	Daniel	Mum	Right pole
1	Weak	3	3	4	7	1	2	3	6	4	6	3	4	2	5	5	3	2	Strong enough to be vulnerable
2	Protective, supportive	6	6	5	1	7	7	6	2	5	2	5	5	6	3	4	7	6	Dependent
3	Sensitive to criticism	3	2	4	7	1	2	3	3	2	4	2	3	2	2	3	1	2	Can cope with criticism
4	Socially confident	6	4	2	2	7	6	4	3	3	2	6	7	6	4	5	3	2	Socially insecure
5	Direct, upfront	6	6	2	1	6	4	6	2	2	4	4	3	2	3	4	6	2	Devious, manipulative
6	Need to be in control	5	3	2	4	7	6	4	2	3	3	6	5	4	3	6	1	2	Let others take the lead
7	Intense	6	2	2	6	2	2	4	3	3	6	3	4	3	2	2	2	1	Relaxed
8	Articulate	1	1	4	1	2	6	2	2	3	1	4	5	4	3	2	1	3	Inarticulate
9	Fears making mistakes	3	2	2	7	1	4	3	4	5	5	2	1	2	2	3	1	2	Accepts making mistakes
10	Shrewd business-wise	4	1	2	1	6	3	2	2	6	1	5	5	5	3	5	1	2	Gullible
11	Unprepared for life	2	1	6	7	1	2	6	6	1	6	1	3	2	5	2	1	1	Prepared for life
12	Angry with life	5	1	5	7	1	1	5	6	2	7	3	4	3	5	4	1	2	Accepting, understanding, coping . . . –
13	Needy, demanding	5	2	5	7	1	1	4	6	2	6	3	4	2	5	5	1	2	Giving, tolerant
14	Afraid of not measuring up	6	3	4	7	2	3	4	6	4	6	3	3	4	4	6	1	2	Accepting shortcomings

Figure 8.1 *Jade's rated grid*

when she first came but wants to be really relaxed. Further change here would certainly bring further improvement in her voice.

Computer analysis brought out 'angry with life' versus 'accepting, understanding, coping with life' as the most meaningful construct (the one with the highest number of other constructs related to it and therefore the most highly elaborated). She had been surprised by how many of the important people in her life *were* angry: her mother, Daniel, Eileen, Mary, Alex, a former boyfriend, her brother Ivan, Derek, her stepfather and Michael, another boyfriend. Looking back she wondered just how much of her energy had been spent in trying to make things better for all these people! Looking at the other pole, the theme of 'acceptance' was clearly important in other dimensions too.

The profile of Daniel, with its extreme negative ratings, expresses the change from her earlier sense of being torn between wanting to protect him and admiring him for his skills and her current feeling that she had no time for him any more. Jade was very thoughtful about her rating of her mother. Although she was 'weak', 'dependent', 'sensitive to criticism', 'fears making mistakes', 'unprepared for' and 'angry with life', 'needy' and 'demanding' she was also 'socially confident', something for which Jade had always been in awe of her. She had been unable to rate herself on this dimension when we first began working but felt that she was 'getting there'.

Jade felt that doing the grid had been useful and clarifying and a fitting end to the work we had done together. She said that in some ways she would like to go on coming 'for ever' but was clear that this was not necessary – it would just be 'an indulgence'. We had both enjoyed the sessions and said so. We agreed that she could contact me any time in the future if there was something she wanted to look at or if her voice deteriorated. She knew that she had more to do to preserve it from the rigours of her intensity and resolved to find some means for working on it. I had suggested the Alexander technique some time ago and she said that she would get in touch with a teacher in her area.

Summary

The subject of this chapter has been the voice and its disorders. I have outlined how things can go wrong, through lack of development, misuse or illness. I have also suggested the psychological effects of dysphonia and some of the approaches to their alleviation. The account of work with Jade illustrates some of the issues which arise when a person sees counselling as a useful means for overcoming the problems which led to her difficulty.

Chapter 9 is concerned with people who suffer speech and language problems due to neurological illness. The range of impairment is described and the impact of that impairment on clients and their families stressed. The chapter ends with an account of work with a dysphasic man and his wife.

9

Counselling People with Neurogenic Communication Problems

In Chapters 7 and 8 the focus has been on working with people who have experienced communication problems, perhaps over many years, perhaps for a relatively short time, which have to some extent influenced their approach to life and their sense of themselves. For them the emphasis is on finding alternative ways of dealing with aspects of life and relationships and on modifying some of their self-perceptions. Change is experienced as a gradual process and there is always a choice as to whether or how far to change.

Where a person suffers from neurological disease or brain damage, there is no choice. In Chapter 1 the effects of loss of control and competency together with deterioration in speech which come with illnesses such as multiple sclerosis, motor neurone disease or Parkinson's disease were described briefly. The shattering impact of sudden loss of abilities after a stroke are outlined. Counselling here will have different aims from work with those who are dysfluent or dysphonic. The emphasis will be on helping the person not only to maintain or restore communication as far as possible but also to maintain or restore some sense of personhood and self-worth.

The range of difficulties in neurological impairment

Brief mention was made in Chapter 1 of dysarthria and dysphasia. In the former, speech may suffer varying degrees of unintelligibilty through weakness, spasticity or discoordination of the muscles controlling breathing, voicing and articulation. In severe cases there may be difficulty with eating and swallowing. Dysphasia is an umbrella term for problems with understanding and expressing spoken and written language. The person may have little or no comprehension or have limitations in the processing of complex language or material of any length. On the expressive side, there may be word-finding difficulty, difficulty with structuring sentences or with following through a train of thought aloud. Where there is also dyspraxia, which may be described as a disorder of motor speech programming, the person cannot produce the appropriate sounds for coherent speech.

These speech and language problems seldom occur alone. Progressive neurological disease can affect the whole body, with paralysis of the limbs and other functions increasing with time. In association with dysphasia there is also often some degree of paralysis of the right side of the body and perceptual difficulties can further disturb any of these clients' ability to relate to things. Emotional lability and various forms of loss of control may be evident at least in the early stages after a stroke or increase over time in progressive conditions. In the latter, too, the person may become more vulnerable to chest and other infections.

The range of personal experiences

One central aim in counselling people in these situations will be for us to understand the meaning of what is happening to them. Assumptions are made about feelings of confusion, anger and despair, which may largely be based on our interpretations of non-verbal behaviour, together with anything that they are able to tell us about how they feel. Working with a particular person over time will hopefully give us the opportunity to gain a fuller impression of an individual experience. It is heartening that today, both in written articles and television programmes, far more attention is paid to the personal experience of a range of disabilities. The popularity of Stephen Hawkings's book, *A Brief History of Time* (1988) also aroused an interest in how this remarkable man has dealt with motor neurone disease. His account of his life detailed in a television documentary is both moving and inspiring.

A number of people who have suffered strokes have recovered sufficiently to write about it. Douglas Ritchie's *Stroke: A Diary of Recovery* (1960), was one of the earliest of these accounts and gave many people insight into what had previously only been described from the outside. In a book devoted to the experience of dysphasia from the inside (Edelman and Greenwood, 1992) a group of people describe what it was like from their first realization that something was wrong, through the frustrations of being unable to make themselves understood, to the time when they have to acknowledge that they have probably reached the limit of their recovery. An excerpt from a poem written by a dysphasic woman (1992: 16) speaks for itself:

Semi-skilled milk.
Hamshit.
Jumbly words and wrongs where rights should be.
Gaps where words should be. And wrongs tensed.
Senses back to front and puzzles expressions
trying to understand my thoughts . . . thoughts
clear as bells but come out so muffled and jangled.
Yes for nos and whole nos have gone.
And whole words die and
Friends say it doesn't matter.
It matters for me. The frustration is intense
and painful and makes me feel so mad and crazy . . .

In a recent lecture on depression associated with dysphasia Borenstein (1993) showed from his research that depression is much more common in strokes where there is loss of language function than where physical disabilities only result. Even a group of young quadriplegic people showed less depression than those who were dysphasic. He believes strongly that 'These people need psychological help, time spent listening and explaining, counselling and basic information.'

Family involvement

One big difference in working with clients with neurological impairments in contrast to adults who stutter or have voice problems lies in the involvement of other members of the family, especially the spouse. The sudden need to be very dependent on a husband or wife has been referred to in Chapter 1 as an issue for many couples. Sometimes a grown-up daughter or son takes on a large share of the caring and where there are younger children still at home the effects on them of a parent's incapacity can be profound. I have found nothing in the literature about these effects but have seen from my own experience how children can mourn, become angry and difficult or withdrawn and isolated.

Sparkes (1993) focuses on the impact of language loss on marriage. In her review of studies of two-person relationships she refers to a number of authors who stress the need not only for couples to share ideas and beliefs but also to communicate with one another about changes in attitudes and the effects these may have on the relationship itself. In their study of the effects of dysphasia on marital relationships Williams and Freer (1986) found that the areas of emotional support, life-styles and sexual relationships were those most severely affected by the trauma. Sparkes suggests that 'in addition to the specific areas noted being intrinsically reliant on communication, the loss of the ability to discuss these areas within the relationship, due to a communication difficulty will exacerbate the changes the two partners are experiencing' (1993: 10).

Social isolation

A whole range of illnesses and disabilities acquired in adulthood can lead to social isolation. One partner may no longer be able to go out and the other be unable or unwilling to leave him or her alone. In most families' experience, the support of friends may be strong at first but dwindles as time goes on. Where there is a communication problem the strain on both visitors and the affected person can become too great. Emotional lability or aggressive behaviour are difficult to handle. Self-help groups may provide the company of others in a similar situation but it is all too easy for a couple's world to become constricted to themselves and close family alone.

Treatment approaches to neurological communication problems

Again in this area, only a representative sample of approaches to the non-psychological aspects of neurological problems will be given. Where there is dysarthria a range of procedures is used, primarily aimed at strengthening the muscles involved in speech: exercises to increase power and control or prevent atrophy; brushing and icing of the tongue and lips to stimulate sensation and movement. Very often the voice too is implicated and attention will be paid to maintaining volume and intonation. It may also be necessary to establish an optimum rate to enable clarity of speech, as in people with Parkinson's disease. Swallowing problems may cause excessive salivation, which will need conscious control or, at their most severe, alternative feeding methods.

Current approaches to the treatment of dysphasia are, like those for dysfluency, wide-ranging and largely dependent on the theories held as to the nature of the problem. Howard and Hatfield (1987), in a highly readable book, group them under a number of headings. These include 'The didactic school', where language skills are retaught, using traditional patterns of teaching reading, writing and grammar to children. 'The stimulation school' believe that by providing the appropriate stimulation the dysphasic person will be enabled to access language abilites that remain, they believe, largely intact but unusable. The approach which has perhaps aroused the greatest interest in recent years is 'The cognitive neuropsychological school'. Here complex theories of language processing have been developed by applying models generated on the basis of laboratory studies of normal subjects to the performance of dysphasic patients. 'The pragmatic school', which appeals to many practising therapists, views the problem more as one of communication than of language and concentrates on developing optimum use of unimpaired abilities to compensate for the language problem.

Psychological intervention with neurogenic communication problems

There is little reference in the literature to the need for attention to the psychological effects of dysarthria in adults. Children with cerebral palsy, which can involve severe speech problems, are seen as socially and emotionally handicapped by their difficulties in communication. Personal accounts of progressive diseases stress the feelings of frustration and loss when speech deteriorates. But writing on the treatment of dysarthria is mainly focused on the physical aspects referred to above. And yet to lose or even suffer impairment in the intelligibilty of speech, together with the changes in resonance and voice which so often accompany it, can have serious effects on a person's life.

Mention was made in Chapter 1 of the woman who spoke only to those she knew well after being described as 'drunk' because of the slurring of her speech. Others have been unable to continue working where communication with the public is involved. Even more damaging is the loss of the ability to express emotions. Even if intelligible speech is possible, lack of inflection, intensity and colour can render the person's utterances lifeless. One man described his situation within the family thus: 'I can tell my wife I love her, but I can't express the feeling of it. I can tick my son off, but he takes no notice of my mumbling.' The use of communication aids has allowed those unable to write or speak to convey something of their meanings to others. There is no aid that I know of which conveys emotions.

People working directly with those who are dysarthric will understand the clients' grief and frustration. Most practitioners will be concerned for what has been lost and some will encourage clients to share their feelings if they wish to. In a group of mainly dysphasic people with whom I worked there was a man with Parkinson's disease, whose speech was quite severely affected. He was very supportive of the others and became quite skilled in interpreting their halting communication. He, however, was regarded as 'the lucky one' as language was intact. Only during individual meetings did he feel able to express his own sense of isolation from his family and friends, being unable to keep up with the lively conversations he had enjoyed so much.

In recent years there has been more consideration of the usefulness of psychological intervention in relation to dysphasic people. Reference was made in Chapter 1 to the recent controversy in some American papers as to whether counselling *or* direct language work was the more beneficial. As with work on dysfluency, it seems unnecessary to choose between direct work and attention to the psychological aspects of the problem. The clinician's choice will be governed first and foremost by the client's wishes. Bryant (1991) uses an approach based on what she calls 'sensory integration therapy and object relations theory' with some elderly patients with communication problems. Here the focus is on sensory experience in such activities as gardening and making music and emphasis placed on the non-verbal responses of individuals. Kalita and Zverkova (1985) found that using role-play with a group of dysphasic people, where action and feeling were called for as well as speech, facilitated verbal communication. Nichols (1993) has researched into the effects of family therapy with dysphasic people. Working with a family therapist she found that the change in attitudes was significant for the dysphasic people themselves and only just short of significant for their families.

Personal construct approaches to neurological impairment

One strong advocate of a psychotherapeutic approach to the management of dysphasia is Brumfitt (1985), whose personal construct work was touched on in Chapter 2. She is mainly concerned with the extent of the person's loss and reactions of grief to the experience. One important finding from her grid study (1985) was that all the people included saw their 'past self' before their illness as very similar to their 'ideal self'. So just as we tend to idealize a lost loved person, the past self becomes, in her words, 'a yearned and longed-for identity and thus idealized'. She sees not only loss of life roles as threatening the sense of self but loss of speech and language abilities, the loss of limb function, as contributing to the confusion as to who they are.

In Dalton (1991), I have considered the effects of brain damage on a person's construing process. It is important for practitioners to take into account the fact that someone with a neurological deficit will be trying to make sense of what has happened to him or her by using a system for understanding which may itself have been greatly changed, quite apart from any speech and language deficits. The *constriction* and tightness of construing which Brumfitt found from her grid study seems inevitable in the face of confusion and threat. Any form of perceptual impairment will blur the person's experience of his or her world. Having to focus on the body to move and balance will contribute to such drawing inwards. Being unable to understand what others are saying or confused as to the meaning of an action or the nature of an object must surely leave the person with a choice between tightening or overwhelming anxiety.

The so-called 'catastrophic reactions' which others find difficult to respond to may be viewed as sudden *dilation* in the face of confusion. What triggers off the burst of anger or grief or seemingly excessive laughter may in itself seem small. But to the person, the strong emotion may well relate to an awareness of far more than we have perceived from the outside. It is not for us to say that the cause is trivial. Only to accept the intensity of the client's experience.

We can only speculate on how a severely dysphasic person construes the future. It has been shown that many idealize their past self. We know that even someone with massive losses will anticipate a future self who is well again and fully recovered. This may be seen as resistance or *hostility* in Kelly's term. But perhaps partial recovery, somewhere in between, with speech and language improved but still not as they were can only be construed through intact linguistic and cognitive abilites. The choice, then, may seem to be between the two extremes of remaining where they are now and a sudden return to where they were before their illness.

Special needs when counselling those with dysphasia or dysarthria

Brumfitt and Clarke (1983) present a model of psychological intervention which recognizes the special needs of those dysphasic people who are unable to use the conventional form of communication in counselling, words. She emphasizes the force of the personal, caring relationship, where the client is receiving full attention from the therapist. It may be that with some people that caring can only be conveyed by tone or touch – or simply *being there*. She refers to the important function of helping the client to express their emotions. She acknowledges how difficult some people find this, seeing it as a sign of weakness, even of disintegration. I agree with her that the release of feelings, especially where they cannot be talked about, can be very valuable and an important indication of trust in the counsellor. But it is important to recognize the meaning of weeping in particular to each client.

Some men especially, but some women too, will not thank you for helping them to cry. Their stiff upper lip in the face of pain may be absolutely central to their sense of themselves. So while our capacity to accept the expression of grief or rage is essential, so is our capacity to accept the person's choice not to show any emotion. However, there can still be a tacit understanding that the counsellor knows something of how the client feels.

Green (1986), came to similar conclusions about his and his colleagues' roles in helping their adolescent clients who had suffered brain injuries. He describes what they were doing in terms of 'sympathetic listening and demonstrated commitment'. Because they were accepting, they were accepted by the young men. He sees them not as advising the young people how to reconstruct their lives but acting as 'evolutionary companions' along the way to whatever recovery was possible for them. They were companions in an experiment and 'maybe the fruits of that experiment can be the rediscovery of a little dignity and a little hope' (1986: 6). This clearly expresses what the counsellor's role may be with older people in these situations.

Some procedures for facilitating communication

One or two examples were given in Chapter 3 of means for establishing non-verbal channels of communication between client and counsellor. Drawing has been referred to in working with both children and adults and the use of objects to convey the meaning of a situation. Accessing a client's meanings is central to many approaches to counselling, not least personal construct counselling. Although Brumfitt and others have shown that it is possible to modify grid technique for clients with communication problems I am more concerned here with eliciting the severely dysarthric or dysphasic person's construing in an ongoing way during counselling sessions, with no particular aim of leading to a grid.

Where clients have adequate comprehension but little or no useful speech it is possible to explore how they see their world of people and themselves using photographs of family and friends. Sometimes a client will suggest through facial expression and gesture some attribute when asked what each person is like. The counsellor can tentatively offer a verbal interpretation of what he or she is trying to convey. Or, from looking at the photograph, suggest that this person seems 'thoughtful' or 'cheerful' or 'anxious'. The contrast poles can also be suggested, but it must be in such a way that the client feels in control of choice and able to reject a label which does not feel right. When a sample of acceptable constructs have been elicited, the client can then 'rate' each person on them, including him- or herself. Thus a profile of the important people in the client's life can be obtained and, most important, a self-profile.

The elements in such a procedure can be made up from anything that it would be useful to explore with the client. They may be situations that have to be dealt with currently – being with the family, among a group of friends, involved in some activity, out among strangers, in various contexts in the hospital. The counsellor might ask clients how they feel in such situations, which they can often convey non-verbally. Unable to speak directly of the things they are passionately interested in, 'dialogue' of a kind can take place through means of this sort.

For people with severe loss of comprehension it is possible to use visual material to elicit something of their feelings about things. I produced a series of photographs designed to express different moods and states – happy versus miserable, angry versus calm, tense versus relaxed, interested versus bored, rejecting versus welcoming, and so on. Those, of course, were my labels and I made no assumption that in putting these pictures into pairs anyone else would make the same contrasts. It has proved possible, though, for quite severely dysphasic people both to tune into the notion of contrast and make their own pairings. These have then been used in conjunction with photographs of people who are important to them. The photographic contrasts are placed apart on the table and the picture of wife, father, daughter or whoever, can be set down close to one pole or the other. In this way clients are again enabled to convey some idea of how they see different people and, especially, what sort of a person they feel themselves to be.

Drawing may not be possible for some clients with upper limb involvement or perceptual problems. But for others it can be a less stressful means of communicating than speaking or writing. They can perhaps draw how they feel at the moment and, however crudely, a picture can express things very vividly, as with the client referred to in Chapter 4 who showed how he felt in relation to his wife and his son. One of the therapists on a counselling course used Ravenette's 'A Drawing and its Opposite' (see page 24) with a group of dysphasic people and found that it led to their sharing their feelings as they had never done before.

The most powerful medium of all for sharing is music. Listening to music together can form a bond of feeling and understanding like nothing else for some. I was told off as a student for 'not doing speech therapy' when I spent a session with a woman with multiple sclerosis and her husband listening to a tape I had made of music she was no longer able to go and hear. It was probably the most fruitful session we had, however, as it reminded them both of what they could still enjoy together despite so much that they had lost. It was also, apparently, the first time that they had allowed themselves to show sadness together.

This kind of procedure helps the counsellor to understand more about the client and gives the client some satisfaction in being able to communicate. And there is at least anecdotal evidence to show that, with the emphasis off the struggle for accurate production of speech and language, dysphasic people often verbalize more freely, quite spontaneously. The same has been found with drawing, where this is possible for clients. Having produced their own non-verbal expression of something which has real personal meaning for them they are then able to find some appropriate words. There are many possible permutations on the ideas suggested, only limited by the limits of our imagination in response to specific need.

Working with David and Sue

The couple and their life together

David and Sue had been married for fifteeen years when he had a stroke at the age of fifty-two. Sue was ten years younger than he and had been married briefly, and disastrously, before. She took a long time to commit herself to another close relationship but the fifteen years had been happy ones. They had no children and lived active working lives. He was a carpenter and joiner and she a junior school teacher. Although not very well off, they were 'comfortable' up until David's illness. They both enjoyed sport and dancing and spent their holidays hill-walking.

Although David had been the more extrovert of the two and more confident, the balance of dependency between them had been healthy, with decisions always jointly made and good agreement as to what they both wanted from life. They had a number of close friends and excellent relations with their parents, who were still alive. They had wanted to have children but Sue wondered whether they would have been a support to her or have made things more difficult.

David had some degree of paralysis down his right side. He could walk with the aid of a stick but his right arm and hand had little movement. His comprehension was good when the input, either in writing or speech, was kept short. Expressive speech, however, was very limited as was writing (with the non-preferred hand) and he often remained silent, rather than struggle to communicate. He had been offered a place at a day centre and attended once. He found others there working on simple carpentry and crafts and Sue felt that the comparison with his earlier skills was too humiliating for him.

Although friendly and clearly a warm personality he was undoubtedly depressed and could become very angry, feeling guilty afterwards if he upset anyone. He had done well working for himself before the stroke but had little money coming in now. Sue believed that he was ashamed of being dependent on her financially and in other ways. She continued to work full-time, coming home at lunch-time to prepare a meal and David spent most of the days alone, although friends had kept him company during the first few months.

Sue was clearly exhausted and David well aware of it. He did his best to help in the house but felt useless. When we spoke together alone Sue said that she did not mind working and running the house but found David's depression draining. She seldom went out with friends and had 'given up' inviting them round, never sure what mood David would be in. There was no doubt in my mind that they cared a great deal for each other but it seemed unlikely that they communicated this to one another. David had apparently lost interest in sex and Sue was too tired to be concerned about that aspect of their lives.

The contract

We first met about a year after David's stroke. They were referred to me by a speech therapist who was no longer able to offer them help, due to cut-backs in the service. She was concerned about the effects the situation was having on the couple's relationship and suggested to them that while I could continue to help David with his speech they both might benefit from working with someone on the difficulties they inevitably had in coming to terms with the enormous change in their lives. David was apparently dubious about this, but hoped for further improvement in his speech and so agreed. Sue at first seemed to regard the proposed sessions as mainly for David, to help him with his feelings of frustration and depression, which had increased over the past year.

The most important aim to me was to re-establish communication between the two. But I felt that this would be better accomplished if, to begin with, I worked with them separately for a time. I suggested that David and I should have some sessions during the day while Sue was teaching and that I should see Sue after school. Later we would work together. I wanted to explore how each of them felt about their situation and find some way of helping them to share what was happening to them in a more fruitful way.

Working with David

My aims here were:

1   To establish optimum channels of communication between us, to be shared with Sue as soon as possible.
2   To explore with him the effects of his situation and help him to find ways of coming out of withdrawal.
3   To find resources for enhancing his life and restoring a sense of his own value.

Channels of communication

I first needed to establish the extent of any comprehension loss and match my language to David's needs. Assessment showed that he could deal with fairly complex spoken language but had a short memory span for what was said. When things were written down he could take in longer communications, as he was able to go back over the material as often as he liked. He had no perceptual problems and could therefore use visual non-verbal material with ease.

I noted early on that expressive speeech was more coherent when it was spontaneous and became far less useful when he struggled to say something. We made an agreement that I would not be demanding speech of him and that he would try to communicate using whatever means occurred to him. When he focused on gesture to convey something, although with one hand only, it seemed to facilitate speech. He was very reluctant to write with his non-preferred hand and at first refused to draw. He had been quite skilled before the stroke and found the crudeness of left-handed drawing shaming. When, however, we had established that this was not an art class he conceded and, in fact, found drawing the most useful channel of expression after a time.

Exploring David's view of himself and his situation

Apart from the logic of first establishing means for communication, the early sessions focused in this way gave us the opportunity to begin a relationship before going more deeply into his feelings about himself. Although Sue had described him as 'open and honest about his feelings' during their time together she had felt him withdraw as the months went by after his illness. He could be angry and sometimes affectionate but hated to show the 'weakness' of tears.

I asked him to draw two contrasting situations – one in which he 'felt OK' and one in which he was 'at his worst'. For the first he drew himself alone to begin with, feet up, watching television. Then he wrote over it 'NO OK'. So I asked him how he would *like* to be. Immediately he sketched himself running. Then I said 'What would be good now?' He thought for a while and slowly drew himself and Sue sitting on a sofa holding hands. I said 'why not?'. He shrugged and pointed to his right arm. This led to a halting conversation about Sue and he conveyed that she would not want to hold his hand now that he was 'no good'. It seemed that he was afraid to touch her in case she rejected him. I asked him whether that might make *her* feel rejected.

When he drew himself 'at his worst' he chose to make a rather bitter joke about it. He was flat on the floor having fallen downstairs. It emerged from Sue that this had happened once during the last year and although he had not hurt himself he felt a fool and Sue had been very frightened for some while afterwards every time he went down the stairs. He had, though, fixed up a rough handrail with a friend of his. This led us to discuss various ways in which he could help himself by using some of the many gadgets available for people with the use of only one hand. He had been offered them at the hospital but dismissed them at the time.

Through many other drawings and some speech I came to understand that David believed himself to be a burden to Sue, that she would be better off without him. He had thought of suicide but knew that that would make things worse for her. He also believed that their friends had written him off and were sorry for what Sue had to put up with. As by now I had talked with Sue I knew that this was not so. They were simply uncertain as to how to be with him. The only people he felt still thought well of him were his own and her parents.

For David to 'restore a sense of his own value' and 'enhance his life' he clearly needed to understand Sue's feelings for him, reconstrue other views of him and take more active steps to involve himself in a new kind of life.

Working with Sue

My sessions with Sue ran parallel with David's. I worked with him twice a week and saw her once weekly. My aims were:

1   To explore the meaning of the situation to Sue and how she felt it had changed their relationship.
2   To see where she could enhance her own life and relieve her exhaustion.
3   To restore her own sense of herself which had also been eroded.

I asked Sue first about the relationship before David's illness. The major dimensions she used to describe it were 'interdependence' versus the 'child-like dependence' she had experienced in relation to her first husband; 'gentleness' versus 'anger', where again the latter characterized her former husband's attitude to her; and 'openness' versus 'shut in'. She summarized their relationship as 'warm friendship plus sexual attraction'. When I asked her to describe it now she had the greatest difficulty. It was as if a number of options were open to them and each was fighting against them. She could be 'motherly' and he sink into a child's role. Although having to make most of the decisions she hated the thought of being 'the boss'. If they could not restore their friendship there was nothing, she felt.

Sue had great difficulty in saying what effects their changed circumstances were having on her. She could put herself into David's shoes and imagine with anguish (and quite accurately I learned) what it must be like for him. It was much harder to look into herself at her own experience. It emerged that one thing standing in her way was a fear of being angry with David. She had every reason to protest at some of his behaviour towards her but deeply feared blaming him for being ill. In her head she accepted that David's outbursts were not really directed at her. But her earlier experiences made it hard for her not to feel hurt by them.

Sue also felt too responsible for his behaviour towards friends, which was one reason why she had not encouraged them to visit. We considered whether she might not be depriving them of the opportunity to show their understanding and acceptance and David of the chance to manage his feelings. When he expressed his misery at 'being a burden' to her she denied it. It took her some time to acknowledge her own sense of deprivation of the life they had lost. She never even admitted to him that she was tired, wanting nothing beyond work for herself.

It seemed clear that it was not only David who needed to express his true feelings. Each was depriving the other of that openness that had been so important to them. Although they could not go back to the same form of interdependence, there were things that both could change in order to restore something of

David's independence. And perhaps gentleness could have its place again if David could redirect the energy of his anger and Sue acknowledge her own needs and more negative feelings.

Working together

After working separately for about a month we agreed on some joint sessions with the following aims:

1 To enhance communication between the two of them.
2 To find ways of increasing David's independence and involvement in things apart from Sue and of extending Sue's constricted way of living.

Changes began to occur before the three of us worked together. Communication between the two of them became easier when David began to use drawing at home. Sue would draw too as well as interpreting David's communications. She realized that she had gradually told David less and less as time went on with the mistaken idea that he would not want her to 'rattle on' when he could not. Now she was coming home and telling him of the day's events and, more important, of how she felt about things.

An important moment in one of our sessions together came when David once again described himself as a 'burden' to Sue. Not wanting to go on denying it Sue did not know what to say. I suggested that 'it', their situation, was indeed a burden and one which they both had to bear. They had every right to feel angry about it. David took Sue's hand and said slowly 'in it together?' This did not mark the end of David's frustration or moments of despair but it seemed to clear the way for other changes.

As he began to trust Sue's feelings of regard and love for him David became more willing to accept that some of his friends at least still valued him. He made a joke of his drawing with them but nevertheless communicated more through it and, as we had found early on, was able to speak more when he relaxed with them. Sue had taken on board the notion that she was being over-responsible with regard to his behaviour with others and learned to step back and let them fend for themselves.

Although David could no longer use many of his manual skills there were things he wanted done in the house and he agreed both to go to occupational therapy to learn to make fuller use of his left hand and to work at home with a friend on the projects he wanted to accomplish. Sue had been reluctant to pursue the sporting activities they had enjoyed without David but he encouraged her to go out more and they began to go to events as spectators together. Their lives would never be the same as before David's illness and their relationship had inevitably undergone change, but I did feel that they had restored some of its most important elements.

Summary

This chapter has attempted to give some idea of the issues that might be involved in counselling adults with neurogenic problems in communication. I have tried to indicate the importance of working with others close to them and the account of work with David and Sue illustrates one way in which a couple may be affected and helped to share their burden together. In Chapter 10 we turn to young childern and their families. Here too the coun- sellor may work both directly with the child on the communication difficulty and with parents and child on the psychological aspects of the problem.

10

Working with Children and their Parents

In Chapter 9 we were concerned with situations where others besides the adult with a neurogenic speech and language problem might be involved. Here the focus is on ways of working with children and those responsible for them. Unlike the adults, most children who come for counselling have not had the experience of speaking for themselves snatched from them, although they may be little used to being heard. They may, in fact, find their views sought and listened to for the first time. On the whole they do not refer themselves. They are referred by parents, teachers or other agencies because of problems of which they may not even be fully aware.

The importance of acquiring communication skills along with other abilities was stressed in Chapter 1. The possible effects on the development of a sense of self where language, articulation, voice or fluency are impaired were described and the need for counselling the children themselves and their families advocated. Here we shall explore aspects of the counselling process as it applies to children with these particular needs.

Special issues when working with children

Although the need for attention to the psychological aspects of communication problems in children is often stressed in the speech and language literature, the details are seldom elaborated. Far more emphasis is placed on the work done with parents to help them follow through treatment plans, modify the environment and resolve any familiy difficulties which might be exacerbating the child's problem. My own understanding of working with children has been enriched by the work of counsellors such as Noonan (1983) and Crompton (1990, 1992), who has a social work background. Many of the issues they address apply to any young people. But there are others which need to be considered in relation to these children especially.

Channels of communication

The first and most obvious is the need for the counsellor to find other channels of communication besides verbal ones with some of the young people. The use of drawing and music is well illustrated by Crompton (1992) and can be vital in work with children with language problems in particular. Some of Ravenette's procedures referred to earlier have been adapted by speech and language therapists for young people who have difficulty verbalizing or who have opted not to speak. A colleague asked a non-speaking child to draw her family and saw clearly how cut-off the child felt. In Dalton and Dunnett (1992) the example is given of how I came to understand a young boy's fears about his body through a drawing he did of himself hiding from other boys during a game.

Observation and inference

Not all children can communicate in this way, however, and the counsellor's skill in observation is especially important here and his or her ability to make inferences from those observations. These must be borne out by further observation, rather than 'interpreted' in the light of some preconceived theory of the meaning of a child's behaviour. In Dalton (1986: 8) a 5-year old who did not speak is described during his early visits:

> No demands were made on him when he came. He could sit quietly with his mother looking at pictures or explore the room and its contents as he wished. The discriminations he was making became clear. He obviously derived considerable satisfaction from the constant repetition of familiar activities which he was happy to share. When confronted with unfamiliar toys he either ignored them or backed away afraid. . . . A picture was emerging of a child whose meaningful world was restricted to a very narrow range. Outside, perhaps, lay chaos . . . I inferred an embryonic construct of himself as someone unable to risk the unknown – anything new threatened this notion. Somewhere along the line it looked as though curiosity and experiment had failed to thrive.

The cause of this situation is not relevant here but through a combination of encouraging the boy to take small experimental steps of his own within a familiar framework and helping the mother to construe him beyond the contrast she had set up between him and his 'devil-may-care' brother, they both began to free themselves from the construction which had hardened around him.

In the case of Ben, referred to in Chapter 3, a problem arose of his being very destructive, loving to throw things and bang them about. His mother was in despair and it had got to the stage where he was only allowed to play in one room in the house. One day when he came with his father I noticed that he was stroking my cat with extreme care. Then he marched up to my room and happily hurled things about as usual. I asked his father whether there were other things which Ben handled carefully. He could only think of the way he approached his baby cousin and a doll that he found in the park and brought home. So Ben did have his own means of discrimination which we could perhaps develop. By picking up and touching certain things with exaggerated care and getting Ben to imitate me and then, in contrast, being quite rough with other things it seemed clear that Ben only needed guidelines to follow. His parents worked on this and deliberately demonstrated with those things which were fragile how he should approach them, instead of shouting when it was too late.

Finding the balance

In Chapter 3 the issue of finding a balance between psychological needs and direct work on the client's communication difficulties is addressed quite fully. With young children the emphasis will more likely be on the latter to begin with, alongside careful listening and observation and acceptance of them as they are. As their ability to communicate improves more direct counselling procedures may be brought in. A further aspect of balancing a programme of work for children lies in the degree of involvement of other people and the forms which that involvement might take.

With small children it is usual to work with a parent or caretaker as a vital part of the sessions. The adults often follow through the speech and language work at home as well as making any adjustments to their handling of the situation which emerge as appropriate. In Dalton (1989) work with 3½-year-old Barry and his mother 'Rosalind' is described, where we functioned very much as a triad, focusing on his speech problem and the intense frustration it caused him. In the case of dysfluent children, whose attention we do not wish to draw to speech, it is more likely that the counsellor will spend most of the time with the parent(s), only seeing the child occasionally for observation. Such work with Caroline and 4-year-old John is outlined in the same paper. With older children, where psychological issues are being addressed more directly, more of the sessions may be with the child alone, with perhaps some joint meetings with parent and child and some with just the adult(s) involved. By adolescence the young person will be the focus of the meetings and the purpose and boundaries of discussions with parents will need to be clearly agreed.

Confidentiality

It is relatively easy to clarify the principles of confidentiality when working with adults. Counsellors undertake to respect all that clients tell them as private, with the proviso that where they feel that clients are likely to be a danger to themselves or others through what they are doing they may, preferably with the clients' knowledge, involve someone else. The situation with children is more complex. Children with communication problems may present even greater dilemmas. If they are used to being dependent on others to interpret and convey their meanings and feelings they may themselves have no notion of privacy and their parents set no boundaries beyond which they will not unthinkingly intrude.

Crompton (1992) shows how easy it is for the counsellor to convey something of how a session has gone simply by the manner in which she hands the child over to the parent. She also points out that in many situations the counsellor has to share something of what has gone on with other colleagues involved with the child, say, in a school setting. It is more often necessary, for the child's protection, to pass on information – about alleged abuse, for example. The important thing is for the child to be able trust the counsellor when he or she says that something will remain private and to be helped to understand when something needs to be passed on.

Crompton quotes Shapiro (1984: 10) as suggesting that:

> Children are used to being talked about by people who care for them; it happens all the time with their parents, and they can accept this as a part of life. They do not necessarily distrust the therapist who also talks to their parents, as long as the therapist's intentions are clear from the beginning of treatment.

And this would seem to be the point. The counsellor needs to negotiate clearly *with everyone concerned* what the 'rules' are. The child needs not only to be sure of privacy but also, perhaps, even to learn for the first time that there is such a thing as confidentiality. The parents may be used to being told everything and find it hurtful or threatening to think of their child saying things, perhaps about them, that they are not to hear. Where the practitioner is both working on communication and counselling the child it must be made clear what aspects of the sessions it would be relevant and useful to pass on to others: some new approach to fluency, perhaps, or some exercises which the child will need to practise at home.

Other aspects of parental involvement

The need to find a balance of parental involvement in terms of the child's age and communication needs has been indicated above. It should be said, however, that with very young children especially, who may not yet be greatly troubled by their language delay, for example, the parents' psychological needs may be the greater and counselling sessions be largely for them. Reference was made in Chapter 1 to the anxiety, guilt and resentment experienced by some parents and other members of the families of children with handicaps of any kind. Ben's mother was an example of one who could not come to terms with her child's retardation and, in fact, refused any help for herself. Others, however, are glad to have the opportunity not only to discover how they can help but to express their fears and negative feelings about the situation.

I have referred often to the need to understand the clients' theories about their problems and it is equally essential to know the parents' views on the meaning of their child's difficulties. They may believe that the child has inherited an impairment or blame themselves for some early trauma which they might have prevented. One mother felt that her child's retreat into silence was due to the birth of her second child. As a result she smothered her first-born with attention and neglected the infant. A father regarded any disability as a sign of 'weakness' and rejected his dysfluent young son. It later emerged that the father had stuttered and been bullied for it by his own father. He needed to break the pattern of this family attitude which was undoubtedly affecting the boy's confidence in himself.

A counsellor may be able to help parents to ease the burden of guilt they feel, especially in relation to inherited problems. By focusing on the here and now and the contribution they can make to the situation as it is, they may cease to apportion blame to themselves or to one another or to 'the doctors'. This may leave them freer to attend not only to the child but also to siblings and to their own well-being. Much more difficult is the task of facing the realities of lasting handicap, instead of searching endlessly for the 'cure' that they believe *must* exist. Helping them to construe their child more fully as the individual that he or she is, rather than the problems presented, is essential here. It can be helpful to ask parents to write a description of the child's experience of a typical day by putting themselves in the child's shoes in an attempt to try to see things through his or her eyes. They may come to realize how different the child's perspective is from their own.

The range of problems in the communicatively impaired child

In Chapter 1 a range of communication impairments found among children was described. The effects of such difficulties on the developing sense of self were particularly stressed. These are likely to be the overriding focus of counselling with young people. Here some means for redressing the balance of negative self-perceptions are suggested, together with procedures for helping them to construe others more clearly and relate to them more effectively.

Negative self-perceptions

Perhaps the most common negative self-perception among these children and one which is continually reinforced by their peers in particular is that they are *unintelligent*. Children who are unable to express themselves verbally, whose speech is hesitant or whose articulation is deviant may well have average or above average intelligence. And yet their inability to show their understanding of things or to voice their ideas, together with the atypical impression of voice or speech pattern will lead not only other children but teachers and parents to regard them as 'not very bright'. Once this notion is set, such a child will become resigned to it, cease to try to compete and settle for underachievement as the line of least resistance.

Working with adults has shown me how these early attitudes may persist into later life. I recognized the all too familiar signs of self-deprecation in an 11-year-old girl. Her articulation was slurred and excessive nasal resonance added to the lack of clarity of her speech. At junior school she had done well and was much encouraged by one particular teacher. A term into her new school, however, and everything seemed to fall apart. She was not doing her homework and had truanted several times. At first she maintained that the homework was 'too hard'. But it emerged that she was made anxious by a less structured way of working and was afraid to ask at the new school when she was not clear as to what was wanted. She had had a few friends at the old school but here, it seemed, from the first day, a boy had begun to mock her speech and 'everyone else' had followed, making her a scapegoat. The confidence she had gained during the last year or so was too fragile to withstand such treatment and she was angry, depressed and apparently at odds with her parents at home.

We needed to restore the sense of her own competence, find some way of handling the bullying and bring her out of her angry withdrawal. The first was the least complicated procedure. She agreed to make sure that she understood what was wanted from the homework and found that when she ventured to ask she could go ahead and get on with it. The bullying took longer to deal with but when we explored that first day more fully it seemed that by no means 'everyone else' had joined in. She had been so upset, however, that she had lumped the whole class together as tormentors and responded badly to any overtures. When she had discriminated between those who had been unkind and those who were not involved she began to speak to some of the latter and gradually to join in with them. The troublesome boy was then hauled up for beating a younger lad and, as is the way of things, lost his ascendancy. The immediate crises being over we then had time to build on her feeling of achievement, develop her rather fragile understanding of friendship and turn our attention to improving her speech.

The view of oneself as *dependent*, even 'helpless' can be hard for many children to shake off. Those with a communication problem may be even more entrenched in patterns of looking to others to speak for them, decide for them and of setting up their parents, siblings and friends as more competent and therefore more responsible than themselves. In some ways it makes for an easier life. It also detracts from the child's potential. Because of a communication problem a child may hang back from many everyday interactions and lack not only the skills but the experience of fending for themselves. If mother has always asked for things in shops or answered the telephone or spoken for the child to teachers, family members and strangers, the child will not know how to begin. A counsellor may need to start from scratch in helping the young person to relate to a whole range of people and events.

Together with a limited view of themselves come unelaborated views of other people. They may take it for granted that other children have no social anxieties and be insensitive to the burden they are placing on a sibling or parent with their demands for reassurance. Nor *will* they understand while their families continue to protect them too much and fail to encourage them to venture for themselves. As adults, they become the 'victim' clients who, in my experience, are so difficult to help. In sessions with such young people it is important to help them not only to find their own resources but to recognize that other people also find things difficult and scary.

However, it can be the case that a child *has* to be dependent on others for some things, for example, if physically handicapped or having insufficient speech to express needs and wants. Here the principle is still the same – to facilitate the child to do as much for him- or herself as possible. But, at the same time, any help that has to be given needs to be offered in such a way that does not make the child feel helpless. Kelly (1955) stresses the idea that dependency is not in itself a negative thing. We need, he says, to spread our dependencies appropriately – know to whom to turn for what. A child who needs assistance is less likely to feel a burden if it is possible to call upon a range of people. A mother who allows no-one else to feed or lift or communicate for her child is setting up a constricted situation which it will be difficult for them both to break out of.

A negative self-perception which may develop, especially around adolescence, is the notion of being *unattractive*. The idea that they 'sound ugly' or 'odd' can pervade the young people's sense of how they are seen by others as a whole. A young girl with a severe stammer drew a picture of herself looking into a cracked mirror. She firmly believed that the facial movements which accompanied her speech blocks made her 'hideous'. Even when she was able to eliminate the movements she seemed reluctant to acknowledge that she 'looked OK'. I have referred to the doubts that young males may have about their sexuality when their voices fail to mature. Some of them feel unattractive to girls and are shy of approaching them. A 12-year-old who described her speech as 'jumbly' also felt that boys and girls alike 'did not take to her' as a person. In working with young people such as these it is not a matter of reassuring them that they are attractive but helping them to develop a better understanding of others' needs and uncertainties as well as of their own and thus gain validation of themselves for who they are.

Children come to feel themselves *unacceptable* for many different reasons. It is not just through awareness of some impairment. It is most often because they feel themselves to be unloved and unlovable. They may fix on their handicap as the reason for this but rejection for any child is far more complicated. A counsellor will see such a fundamental negative self-perception as central to everything he or she attempts to do to help. Whether it is ever possible to erase the effects of not being loved by parents I do not know. But experiencing, perhaps for the first time, the counsellor's unconditional regard and respect for what is important to them may be the first step in a process of healing which many children need.

Children referred with 'behaviour problems' seem sometimes to be working very hard at confirming their reputation for 'badness'. One 13-year-old boy had been thrown out of two schools for unruly behaviour. His parents were at their wits end and brought him to me because it had been suggested that he might have a mild form of autism involving language and perceptual difficulties. His mother said that she 'tried hard' to love him. His father dutifully sought what help there was but wished that the boy had never been born. The boy refused any attempts at language assessment and sulked for about half an hour at our first meeting. Then I tried Ravenette's approach of focusing on the child's expertise. His happened to be good at computer games and kickboxing. He described the first and began to demonstrate the second. Fortunately he was very skilled and although his blows came horribly near to my defenceless head he did not actually strike me.

A child may be intelligent and feel stupid. He or she may not be very bright but feel accepted as they are. The degree of children's dependency will come partly from the way they are treated by their families and partly from what they make of that treatment. The issue of attractiveness will be central to some young people but not to others. To know that we are loved is essential to us all and governs our capacity to relate to others.

Working with Michelle and her parents

The family

Michelle was a 12-year-old when we first met. Her language development had been quite severely delayed but skilled professional help and enormous support from her parents had enabled her to cope well in a mainstream school during the past year. Her father, Jon, managed a small bookshop and her mother, Marion, worked as a secretary for a firm of solicitors. Her brother, Tom, was two years younger. They lived in a small flat in north London, near to Marion's parents, who were closely involved in their lives.

Exploring the presenting and underlying problems

Meeting the parents
Jon and Marion, a couple in their early thirties, first came to see me on their own. Jon was a serious, intense man who was keen

for me to understand the urgency of their concern. Marion was more relaxed in herself but equally anxious to get help for their child. They were worried about Michelle, but not quite sure what help she needed now. They described her as tense, anxious and often irritable and were afraid that her difficult start as far as communication was concerned had undermined her confidence. The teachers at school found her difficult and she did not make relationships with other children easily. She was extremely jealous of her brother. He was very bright, good-natured and unshakable in his devotion to her however she treated him.

Although she was 'keeping up' at school, written work remained more difficult for her than maths or other less verbal subjects and she could become very frustrated when unable to manage things. They hoped, therefore, that I could give her more help with language. Jon in particular, though, saw the child's anxiety and difficulty with people as more important and stressed the need for 'counselling'. I agreed to see Michelle and let them know how I might help her. They had not told her that they had come to see me and had in mind to tell her that I might help her with her school work. I was not happy with this and the false expectations such an explanation might set up. I suggested that it would be better to tell Michelle that they had talked to me and let her know of the sort of work I did with people. She could come to meet me and see whether she felt comfortable talking to me. If she did then we could sort out issues of confidentiality between us.

Meeting Michelle

Marion brought Michelle to see me a few days later and left us together. Michelle was undoubtedly anxious but presented herself as rather bored with the whole thing and not about to fall over herself to please me. I asked her why she thought she was here and she shrugged her shoulders. Did she think she needed help with anything? Her English, she supposed. Did anything else trouble her? Not really. Who was concerned about her then? Mum and Dad. Why? She didn't know. I then asked her what she really enjoyed doing. Nothing much – except sport. And painting sometimes.

I then said that I was going to ask her some questions which would help me get to know her a little to see whether there was anything we could work on together. I asked her first to tell me three things in answer to 'Who are you?' She looked surprised and laughed but said: 'I'm Michelle, I'm a girl, I go to St Mary's.'

[P.D. = Peggy Dalton; M. = Michelle]

P.D.: Is it important that you are Michelle?
M.: Not really. I could be anybody.
P.D.: Would you like to be somebody else?
M.: I'd like to be somebody clever.
P.D.: Is it important that you are a girl?
M.: I wouldn't want to be a boy!
P.D.: How important is it that you go to St Mary's?
M.: [Immediately] Very. I was at the special school before.
P.D.: What sort of a person are you? Tell me three things.
M.: I'm good at sport, especially running. I don't like school dinners. I don't have any friends.
P.D.: Is being good at sport important to you?
M.: Of course.
P.D.: Are school dinners important?
M.: They're boring.
P.D.: How important is it that you don't have any friends?
M.: Sometimes I don't care. Sometimes I do.
P.D.: When does it matter?
M.: Always really.

Picking out what seemed to be of most concern to her I asked her whether I was right in thinking that she wanted to get on well at St Mary's, both with her work and with the other girls. She said yes. Would she like to talk to me about any difficulties she had with work and the teachers, perhaps? And how would it be if we tried to sort out why she had no friends? She said 'OK'. I then said that I hadn't any paints but would she draw something? 'OK' (but she looked quite enthusiastic). The rest of that session she spent drawing a number of pictures related to a recent holiday. The focus was on the sea and the beach, on boats and the house that they had rented. She said nothing about the holiday itself.

The plan of action

It was agreed between us all that Michelle should come for six sessions and that the focus should include both her work and issues to do with relationships. The sessions would be 'private' and only if I felt it would be helpful to discuss anything with her parents would I put it to her that I should do so. At the end of the six sessions I would meet her parents again. Anything they talked about would also be 'private'. If they all wanted the sessions to continue we would agree together where we went from there.

Relating to work
Michelle had had a good deal of expert help with language for

many years and her progress fully justified integration into a mainstream school. Her skills in verbal expression were adequate, both in writing and speech. She had some difficulty in abstracting the important points from reading and occasionally lost the thread when too long an explanation of something was given verbally. There was no doubt that she was keeping up, however, and the main problem was her fear of failure, especially in a test situation. We reviewed how far she had come over the years and what her strengths were now. Although everyone had assured her that a language problem did not mean lack of intelligence, when I put it to her that it took real intelligence to overcome a language problem she seemed surprised and pleased.

She clearly needed a new way of relating to school work and we looked at ways of reducing her anxiety and helping her to value her achievements. I asked her which was best – to try to be top in class, to be at the bottom or to be in the middle. She knew what I was after and said that being in the middle was best – trying to be top was 'too hairy' and being at the bottom 'too dim'. In order to stay in the middle she needed to work steadily and organize her work, instead of either sitting at it for hours or giving up in a temper after five minutes. She often came home without the materials and details she needed, so the first priority was to get organized. Each week we planned ahead in terms of the optimum time to spend and the books and other resources she would need. This in itself reduced the anxiety. Like all her classmates she was very mark-conscious, but I got her to evaluate her work on other counts too, such as whether she was attempting something new or how easy or difficult others had found it.

Relating to people

As these early sessions went on we were spending less and less time on the issues around work. Relationships with others and her views of herself took precedence. It became clear that she felt loved and valued by her parents, although she had some difficulty in expressing her affection for them. Her suspicions about the teachers and her sullenness with them related to her anxieties about work and as these lessened she began to experience them as less threatening. The main problems were with her peers and we began by exploring her relationship with her brother.

She grudgingly admitted that he was, in fact, 'OK', but her jealousy of him made her very ambivalent towards him. Two years younger than herself, he was ahead of her in many things. Although the parents had been careful not to compare the two in this respect, Michelle herself clearly did and found herself wanting.

He also excelled in sport, which was galling to her. He was very popular with both adults and children and this was the worst thing of all. At first I tried to help her see the two of them as 'just different', rather than the one 'better' than the other, but she wasn't having any of that. It wasn't fair. I left him for the moment and went on to other relationships.

Why did she think she had no friends? The familiar shrug. What did other people do who had friends that she didn't do? No idea. So we set about unravelling the mysteries of friendship. The first thing that became clear was her failure even to try to imagine how other people saw things. It is probable that her difficulty with language gave her a bad start here. When she described incidents at school she could only see them from her own perspective. I put forward some suggestions about how other people possibly experienced them and she 'supposed' I might be right. Only when we began to use role-play did she begin to put herself in someone else's shoes.

I also used Ravenette's 'Perceptions of Troubles in School' pictures (1977). Here various situations in school are drawn in such a 'fuzzy' way that they are open to interpretation. The exercise is aimed at exploring how typically a child might deal with the situations as he or she construes them. The pictures showed me how defensively Michelle approached them, seeing themes of rejection and misunderstanding in a number of them. But they were also useful for elaborating the part other people might play in the situations: 'If you did that, what might that girl feel?' 'What do you think the teacher would think if you said that?' She enjoyed this and it seemed that she *was* able to use her imagination when an idea was put to her.

A session with Jon and Marion

Michelle expressed no concern when the time came for me to have the agreed session with her parents. She hoped we could go on. Marion began by expressing pleasure that Michelle seemed to be getting on better with her work and seemed happier generally at school. Jon agreed but said that things were not really improved at home. I tried to get them to pin-point more clearly what was wrong. Again they referred to Michelle's jealousy of Tom. I acknowledged that so far I had got nowhere with that. And, although she got on well with her grandmother and behaved well with her, she was rude and sullen with her parents. Why did they think this was, apart from her feelings about Tom. Marion thought that in some way she blamed them for the difficulties of her early years. Jon admitted that he and Michelle were very much alike and rubbed each other up the wrong way. He thought a lot of her, though, and wished he could somehow make her understand this. Did he actually tell her? He said 'Yes', but Marion said 'No, not really'. Jon would, he said, try to talk to Michelle sometime when things were calm. Both parents wanted the sessions to continue.

Working on with Michelle
The exercises in role-play and experiments with 'Troubles in School' were potentially useful but obviously not enough. Michelle needed to communicate with the other children more, engage herself with them, listen to them, find out about them and let them know something of herself. This was more difficult. She began to make tentative headway, though. She chose a quiet girl, whom she liked the look of, and asked to sit next to her at lunch. She started to stay behind with the others after games practice, instead of rushing off home. She said that she didn't really know what to talk about but it was 'OK' just being there. There was one near disaster when a girl apparently ignored her and made her feel an intruder in a group, but she decided that she was just rude anyway.

I did not ask Michelle whether she and her father had talked together but it emerged that she had begun to tell her parents about our sessions and what was going on at school. Something had begun to change there. Then, when we had worked together for about three months, something occurred which none of us could have foreseen that changed the direction of the counselling series.

The unexpected

During a short break for their summer holiday the family went with the grandparents to Wales. On their second day there, Tom was climbing a steep hill with his father, slipped and hit his head on a rock as he rolled down the slope. He was taken to hospital but died the next day.

Michelle's father wrote a short note explaining what had happened and postponing my next appointment with her. A few weeks later her mother telephoned and asked if I would see Michelle. She was clearly devastated and said that her husband was blaming himself, saying that he could have prevented the accident. When I asked her what support she had she said that her parents were keeping her sane, although very upset themselves. She was worried about Michelle, who had cried when the accident happened but had said very little and shown little emotion since, except to her grandmother.

A child's experience of grief

Before I saw Michelle a few days later I tried to imagine from my knowledge of her what she might be experiencing now. Her envy of her brother held a good deal of admiration and she might be as ambivalent about his death as she had been about him when he was alive. Her parents' and her grandparents' grief would emphasize the love they had for him, although I was sure that her mother and father would be doing their best to make her feel loved too. I could only speculate on the sort of fantasies she might have had from time to time of being rid of him and having no one to outshine her or compete for her parents' attention. I wondered how much guilt she felt for the way she had been towards him.

When she arrived she seemed quite composed, but rather remote. However, her anxiety began to show itself after a few minutes. She got up from the chair in which she usually sat and moved around for a few minutes before choosing another. It seemed to signal her acknowledgement that she was here for a different purpose. I asked her how she was and she said 'OK'. She was due back at school next week but didn't know whether she would be going just yet. I asked her whether she might find it difficult and she was not sure. Then she said that it was 'awful' at home. I asked her what it was like.

Her main preoccupation was with her parents, especially her father. He apparently hardly spoke and she had heard him crying one night, which shocked her very much. Her mother could not concentrate on things and only her grandmother seemed able to keep things going. I asked her what it was like for her and she said 'very miserable'. Then: 'Mum said I'd have to talk to you about the accident'. I said that she didn't *have* to talk to me about anything but it might be helpful to talk about Tom. Much of what followed was quite disjointed, there were long silences, but she was able to communicate some very powerful and unhappy feelings.

She was very frightened by the effects of her brother's death on her parents. They would never be the same again. Her own feelings were confused and she was shocked that sometimes she just didn't feel anything at all. Her grandmother was the only one she could talk to and she obviously found her a comfort. She missed Tom and wished that she hadn't been so nasty to him. Would everybody have been as upset if she had died instead? She had sometimes imagined dying to make people sorry.

I told her that I had done the same when I was her age but

hadn't really known what it would be like for my family. We looked at how almost all brothers and sisters wished each other harm sometimes but really cared if something bad happened. She then went on to describe the day Tom died. She had not been with him and had stayed behind with her grandparents when they took him to hospital. She was asked the next day whether she wanted to see him and had said no. This obviously worried her, but she had been reassured by her grandmother that that was all right, probably best. Again, it was the effect on her father that day that had shaken her most. I tried to put myself in his place and tell her something of how he might be feeling and why he was shut in on himself now. Her parents *would* never be the same, but it would not always be like this.

It struck me when she left at the end of the session how open and honest she had been about her feelings. Although her account of things was not always coherent there was a maturity about her which was new. She said that she would like to come again to talk some more and work out whether to go back to school yet. We met throughout the autumn, talking about how things were at home, about school, about how her life had changed. She was able to talk more to her mother and to share her grief with her. Her father she described as 'all shut in' and was clearly unapproachable. Christmas was predictably a very bad time for them all and Michelle was quite deeply depressed for some weeks. We sometimes hardly spoke at all in sessions and she only wanted to draw – pictures which told of nightmares, anger and fears. As the new year went on she came out of it and seemed able to look forward again. We began to meet less frequently and had our last session when the anniversary of her brother's death was passed.

I saw her parents once more before the sessions ended with Michelle. I was shocked by how much Jon seemed to have aged and by the obvious depth of his depression. When I asked them how they were he wanted only to speak of Michelle's progress, which he felt was good. He made no reference to any difficulty between them this time, but I had the impression from Marion that he was still very cut off from everyone. I tried again to ask them about themselves and although I think Marion would have liked to talk, Jon brought the meeting to an end. I still ask myself whether I could have done more to help him if I had been more pressing.

Summary

This chapter has been concerned with some of the main issues involved in counselling children and their families. The range of problems which may arise in work with young people with communication difficulties and the various forms parental involvement might take have been outlined. In the final chapter the experience of working in this area from the counsellor's point of view will be the focus.

11

An Experience of Counselling People with Communication Problems

I hope it is implied throughout this book that the experience of counselling is as meaningful for the counsellor as it is for the client. Both are involved in the processes of exploring, experimenting and change. As clients learn more about themselves through reflecting on their experience of things and trying new ways of approaching aspects of life, counsellors also learn – about themselves, about other people and about counselling. Change takes place in both partners in the enterprise. And change occurs in the counsellor over time through the cumulative process of working with a range of people and their problems. I shall begin this chapter with an account of my own professional journey. Not that it has been in any way remarkable. Many counsellors begin as practitioners in one of the helping professions and find, as I did, that their training lacks an important dimension. It may be of interest to some of these colleagues to compare their experience with mine.

A professional journey

My training as a speech therapist prepared me for work with speech, language and voice disorders and, to some extent, taught me to listen to and feel for the people involved. Lectures emphasized the need for accurate diagnosis and appropriate treatment. Placements in hospitals and school clinics as a student reinforced this message but also gave me some insight into the frustrations and limitations suffered by adults and children. At that stage, however, I had neither the understanding nor the experience to take in the deeper layers of need among clients. As a newly-qualified therapist I followed through my assessments meticulously and carried out treatment programmes with conscientious thoroughness.

It was the clients themselves who widened my horizons. They

wanted more. They talked to me and told me of things which my training had not prepared me for. From the beginning I worked with people who stuttered. They were, of course, concerned with fluency and hoped that I would come up with a technique that would 'work'. But they also spoke about their childhoods, the way their parents had handled things, their current problems with relationships and their fears for the future. The parents of children would sometimes tell me of their anxieties, not only for their sons and daughters but for the whole family. When I joined the neurological unit of a large London hospital I felt helpless to ease the confusion and pain experienced by stroke patients and their spouses.

Dissatisfaction

As time went on I became more dissatisfied with what I had to offer people, and more aware that I was only half-equipped to help them. I probably became better at listening and my understanding of a range of experiences grew. But I did not know where to go from there. I began to research a number of psychological approaches with a view to training in counselling and psychotherapy. At first I was attracted to Rogers's client-centred counselling and I still find much in it that I respect. For a while I was drawn to cognitive behaviour therapy and, again, retain regard for that too. Then, with the publication of Fransella's *Personal Change and Reconstruction* in 1972 I met Kelly's personal construct psychology for the first time and knew that I had found what I was looking for.

I began tentatively to introduce the ideas into my work with people who stuttered, the subject of Fransella's study. I found that using self-characterizations gave me more insight into the ways in which clients viewed themselves and their difficulties and Kelly's emphasis on experimentation as a means towards change influenced what I did in relation to the groups I was then running. But it was not until 1978 that I began my training in personal construct psychology, joining the first course for members of the helping professions to be run in this country. (That course is described in Fransella, 1980.)

Confusion

This course and the advanced training which followed changed my approach to speech therapy radically. It was exciting but also threatening. For a time I wondered whether anything that I had done since I qualified had been of any value at all. Colleagues have since told of the same experience of confusion and doubt as old notions were being challenged by new ones. With PCP ideas and procedures barely grasped we have all wondered when and where we should 'apply' them, as if they were some kind of sticking plaster. Was it possible to reconcile the need for direct work with psychological exploration? Time was needed for reflexivity to grow, the process of construing ourselves from a PCP perspective, and for the ideas to become part of our way of looking at life, before we could integrate the best of our understanding of communication problems with this approach to understanding the people who have to cope with them.

Diversification

When I joined Fay Fransella to set up the Centre for Personal Construct Psychology I began to work with clients with a range of problems besides speech and language difficulties. I had encountered depression, anxiety, obsessionality, even, without fully realizing it, psychosis among earlier clients. But this gave me the opportunity to learn about them and work with them more deeply and with the supervision that had never been provided in former environments. It also made me realize how often such problems are either masked or exacerbated by communication disorders. And just how complex an area of work I had been engaged in all those years.

There is no doubt that counselling within a wider range increased my understanding of the experience of people with speech, language and voice problems. But my earlier (and, of course, still ongoing) work also contributed to my understanding of some of my later clients. The parallels, for example, between stuttering and eating disorders were striking. In each situation clients can be obsessed by the one aspect of their being – their dysfluency or their eating behaviour. Both can amount to 'role' problems, where clients construe themselves almost entirely in these terms.

Speech anxiety or the anxiety experienced by people with voice problems is of a very particular kind with its focus being on communication with others. But other anxious people have their own preoccupations with feared events and people and, like them, need, among other things, to change their negative perceptions of themselves. Dysphasic people may be very depressed. They are constricted by their sense of the limitations of their condition and circumstances. All depression is to do with constriction of some kind and many depressed clients may be helped by dilating their view of the world and its possibilities.

There are many reasons for children to become troubled and

troublesome and those with language, speech or voice problems may be more vulnerable in this respect. Working with children with no communication impairment has, in fact, made me more aware of what else can go wrong. It has alerted me also to dangers which may be ignored in our preoccupation with the specific difficulties. Dangers of undispersed dependencies, of labelling a child with some narrow attribute or limiting their potential through our failure to construe the nature of experience for them.

It has been very important to me to work with children *and* adults. And, again, experience with the young has affected my work with older people and vice versa. Any counsellor will know that, at times, clients are very much in touch with the child in them. They will need to revisit old experiences and feel old feelings. Working with young children not only helps me to respond in these situations but keeps me in touch with the child in myself. Listening to people's accounts of their earlier years it is sometimes useful to reflect with them on how an event might have seemed at the time, before greater sophistication brought about the inevitable reconstruction of the past.

Being alongside a child going through a difficult experience I bear in mind what may be made of it later and this gives an urgency to the need I feel for him or her to express an understanding of it as clearly as possible. Parents will all too often assume that a child who says nothing about a bereavement, a divorce or a major life change is therefore attaching no meaning to it. They, therefore, say little or nothing and the child may internalize a sense that he or she is in some way to blame for what is going on. From working with adults I know there is much evidence of deep and lasting harm from misunderstandings of this kind.

Teaching PCP to practitioners from many different areas of work also taught me a great deal. At first, the range of experience of many of my 'students' was wider than mine. I marvelled at their ability to run hostels for severely disturbed people or to grasp the many important strands of community social work or to use art to communicate with confused and deeply unhappy people. But it helped me to dilate my own view of the potential of PCP and to be more inventive in adapting procedures to special needs. As my experience widened I was also able to encourage developments within speech and language therapy beyond the original focus of work with people who stuttered.

Becoming a supervisor was a further opportunity to learn more about clients, about PCP and about myself as a counsellor and psychotherapist. Some members of groups and individuals whom I supervised were more eclectic than I and I became interested through them in what other approaches to counselling had to offer. I read more widely and began to incorporate some aspects of these other approaches which made sense to me within a PCP framework. Supervision, needing to address issues related to clients, to counsellors and to the process of counselling, is perhaps the richest source of all for reflection and learning.

Integration

Through these experiences the confusion of the early years has eased. I no longer ask myself whether I am 'doing speech therapy' or 'counselling' people, when my clients have communication problems. I may need to establish a balance between attention to speech, language or voice and to the psychological aspects of the person's experience. But movement between the two is smooth and clear. Adaptations of procedures for those with speech and language problems have made exploration of people's construing and experimentation more possible. But I have ceased to feel that I am 'not using PCP' if I am unable to ask for a self-characterization or set up a grid or even elicit constructs in some kind of formal way. We can watch for and tune into clients' ways of making sense of things as well as listen for their verbal expression.

Writing this book, where I have had to draw together my understanding and experience of communication problems and of counselling has been in itself an integrating process. I have not until now taken such a comprehensive view of the range of work or of developments over time. I have probably addressed many of the important issues from time to time in discussions with colleagues or in writing. But here I have tried to gather them together and, in the process, asked myself some new questions – about training, about practice and about the degree of awareness of the complex nature of these difficulties among the public at large and those responsible for provision of services.

Training issues revisited

In Chapter 1 I looked at issues of training in terms of the lack of attention to counselling in speech and language therapy training. There is evidence that many therapists are all too aware of this and seek further training in psychological intervention once they are qualified. Other professionals work particularly with those who stutter and with people who have voice problems, and I am not suggesting that they should not. I only feel that counsellors and psychotherapists who do involve themselves with communication problems should seek understanding of every aspect of them, not just the psychological.

Although not all speech and language therapists will wish to take on counselling, I have come to feel very strongly that far more time should be spent on it during training courses. I know that the situation has changed over recent years but still, as we saw, Miller (1990b) found from her survey that while at one college one day a week was given over to it over three years, at another there had been just one one-day course throughout the respondent's period of training. Lectures on psychopathology, as I know from my own experience, are no substitute. Lack of the practical, theoretical and experiential aspects of counselling training has a number of adverse effects.

The most important of these perhaps lies in the absence of supervision. Professionally, newly-qualified therapists are 'supervised' by their seniors. But this does not mean the same as in the area of counselling. The supervisor will be concerned with the work that the therapist is doing with clients but is unlikely to give the young person's own experience of the process the same attention. While experienced counsellors take the need and usefulness of supervision for granted, in many other helping professions there is even hostility towards the idea that it should be necessary. In my own profession, too, among many colleagues, the need for support and to check out what one is doing with clients feels like a 'weakness'. I believe that our growth as practitioners cannot depend only on experience and reading. We need ongoing feedback and challenge if our approach is not to ossify.

I have said that not every speech and language therapist will want to become involved in counselling. And we saw in Chapter 1 that the use of conjoint therapy or referral on to those appropriately trained may resolve the problem of a client's need for psychological help. When working with parents or the relatives of older clients, those wishing to concentrate on communication can also refer the clients to other agencies and support groups. But it is where psychological needs are ignored or the complexities of the communication problem not understood that harm may be done by professionals who are ill-equipped to work in this area.

Public awareness

There has undoubtedly been some increase in recent years in public awareness of communication problems of all kinds and their implications for the people concerned and their families. Various pressure groups have mounted campaigns to inform others of the experience and needs of those who are deaf, who stutter and who fail to learn to speak. Many of the difficulties discussed in these chapters, however, are hidden or not taken seriously by those who have no experience of them. Teachers are now better informed so that in schools more remedial help is given with reading, language and perceptual problems. But teachers too are often unaware of the full implications for the children concerned.

Our current best hope would seem to be with television. People will watch programmes about particular conditions, which are often very well made, and find themselves truly interested in what they learn. A neighbour has a son with motor neurone disease, who became severely physically handicapped before moving to the area. The programme about Stephen Hawkings referred to in Chapter 9 was a revelation to many of those who saw him taken out in his wheelchair and had assumed that he was also severely mentally handicapped. Attitudes towards the mentally handicapped have a long way to go before there is a significant change, but a film of some people with Downs Syndrome rehearsing and performing a play some years ago had a profound effect on many viewers.

Persuading the providers

Unfortunately there has not been a parallel growth in understanding and concern among those who provide services for people with communication problems. The recent establishment of the Michael Palin Centre for Stammering Children moved one government minister to comment on what an excellent job they were doing. But services in the community and in hospitals continue to be 'streamlined' and the urgency for swift 'throughput' of clients has turned the focus even more onto measurable results. Colleagues working with dysphasic people are asked to show that language has increased through treatment, not whether clients are feeling less depressed or relating more easily with their families and friends. We *can* measure changes in people's self-perceptions and in their perceptions of other people. But the forms provided to specify progress in speech, language or use of voice do not allow for grid results, drawings or writing to be taken into account.

Given the current demand for cutbacks and the nature of 'auditing', which is being transferred from goods to people, I can come up with no solution to the present situation. I do not know how you market a service whose results are less tangible than improvements in concrete products. How, too, can we weigh the needs of those suffering painful physical conditions or in need of well-attested operative procedures against the less predictable and less measurable harm that neglect of communication impairment may bring? The waiting lists for hip replacements may be excruciatingly long while those for places in language units for children who are not learning to comprehend or speak are endless. If these children are fit and well or if elderly dysphasic people can be looked after physically at home, their communication needs and their psychological needs will have to wait.

All we can do, I believe, is to make sure that the service we are able to provide is as comprehensive as possible, mindful of every aspect of the experience of communicative impairment. We can try to develop a real understanding of the needs of people in these situations and of those who care for them. Training can always be improved. Practitioners must always go on learning from each other and from their clients. We must be willing to share our knowledge with the rest of society and do what we can to make those in power hear us.

The never-ending journey

There are probably few professions where a person can truly say that they have 'done it all' and that there is no more to learn. Counselling is a process which brings new experience with each new client. We hope that they add something to their understanding of themselves and of life through working with us and we know that they add something to us through working with them. Counselling people with communication problems is a complex and deeply challenging area of work. It is also deeply satisfying.

References

Albert, M. and Helm-Estabrooks, N. (1988) 'Aphasia therapy works', *Archives of Neurology*, 45: 372–3.

Aronson, A.E. (1990) *Clinical Voice Disorders*. New York: Brian C. Dekker.

Beail, N. (ed.) (1985) *Repertory Grid Technique and Personal Constructs*. London and Sydney: Croom Helm.

Beery, Q.C. (1991) 'Psychosocial aspects of adolescent dysphonia: an approach to treatment', *Language, Speech and Hearing Services in Schools*, 22 (3): 163–7.

Borenstein, P. (1993) 'Depression and Aphasia', Ninth Annual Mary Law Memorial Lecture. London, 20 April.

Britton, J. (1971) Introduction to 1971 edition of A.R. Luria and F. Yudovich, *Speech and the Development of Mental Processes in the Child*. Harmondsworth: Penguin.

Brooks, A.R. (1991) 'Behaviour problems and power relationship', *Language, Speech and Hearing Services in Schools*, 22 (2): 89–91.

Brumfitt, S. (1984) 'A personal construct investigation into loss of communicative ability in the aphasic person'. M.Phil. dissertation, Sheffield University.

Brumfitt, S. (1985) 'The use of repertory grids with aphasic people', in N. Beail (ed.), *Repertory Grid Technique and Personal Constructs*. London and Sydney: Croom Helm.

Brumfitt, S. and Clarke, P. (1983) 'An application of psychotherapeutic techniques to the management of aphasia', in C. Code and D.J. Muller (eds), *Aphasia Therapy*. London: Edward Arnold.

Bryant, W. (1991) 'Creative group work with confused elderly people: a development of sensory integration therapy', *British Journal of Occupational Therapy*, 5 (5): 187–92.

Burk, K.W. and Brenner, L.E. (1991) 'Reducing vocal abuse: "I've got to be me"', *Speech, Language and Hearing Services in Schools*, 22 (3): 173–8.

Butcher, P., Elias, A. and Raven, R. (1993) *Psychogenic Voice Disorders and Cognitive Behaviour Therapy*. London: Whurr.

Butler, R.J. (1985) 'Towards an understanding of childhood difficulties', in N. Beail (ed.), *Repertory Grid Technique and Personal Constructs*. London and Sydney: Croom Helm.

Byrne, R. (1987) 'Individual therapy with the very severe stutterer', in C. Levy (ed.), *Stuttering Therapies: Practical Approaches*. London and Sydney: Croom Helm.

Canter, A. (1991) 'A cost effective psychotherapy', *Psychotherapy in Private Practice*, 8 (4): 13–17.

Chabot, B.E. (1988) 'Gesprekshulp', *Jdschrift voor Psychotherapie*, 14 (6): 299–320.

Challoner, J. (1991) 'Gender identity problems', in R. Gravell and J. France (eds), *Speech and Communication in Psychiatry*. London: Chapman and Hall.

Clifford, J. and Watson, P. (1987) 'Family counselling with children who stutter: an Adlerian approach', in C. Levy (ed.), *Stuttering Therapies: Practical Approaches*. London: Croom Helm.

Cooper, E.B. (1987) 'The Cooper Personalized Fluency Control Program', in L. Rustin, H. Purser and D. Rowley (eds), *Progress in the Treatment of Fluency Disorders*. London, New York and Philadelphia: Taylor and Francis.

Crompton, M. (1990) *Attending to Children: Direct Work in Social and Health Care*. Dunton Green: Edward Arnold.

Crompton, M. (1992) *Children and Counselling*. London, Melbourne and Auckland: Edward Arnold.

Cushway, D. and Sewell, R. (1993) *Counselling with Dreams and Nightmares*. London: Sage.

Dalton, P. (ed.) (1983) *Approaches to the Treatment of Stuttering*. London and Canberra: Croom Helm.

Dalton, P. (1986) 'A personal construct approach to therapy with children', in G. Edwards (ed.), *Current Issues in Clinical Psychology*. New York and London: Plenum Press.

Dalton, P. (1987) 'Some developments in individual personal construct therapy with adults who stutter', in C. Levy (ed.), *Stuttering Therapies: Practical Approaches*. London and Sydney: Croom Helm.

Dalton, P. (1988) 'Personal construct psychology and speech therapy in Britain: a time of transition', in G. Dunnett (ed.), *Working with People*. London and New York: Routledge.

Dalton, P. (1989) 'Working with mothers and children: a personal construct approach', *Clinical Psychology Forum*, 23: 3–6.

Dalton, P. (1991) 'Reconstruing the self after brain-damage', paper presented at the 1st Speech, Language and Counselling Conference. London, 11 July.

Dalton, P. and Dunnett, G. (1992) *A Psychology for Living*. Chichester, New York, Brisbane, Toronto and Singapore: John Wiley.

Davis, H. and Cunningham, C. (1985) 'Mental handicap: people in context', in E. Button (ed.), *Personal Construct Psychology and Mental Health*. London, New York and Sydney: Croom Helm.

De Pompei, R. and Zarski, J.J. (1989) 'Families, head injury and cognitive-communication impairments: issues for family counseling', *Topics in Language Disorders*, 9 (2): 78–89.

Dryden, W. (ed.) (1992) *Hard-earned Lessons from Counselling in Action*. London: Sage.

Dunnett, G. (ed.) (1988) *Working with People*. London and New York: Routledge.

Edelman, G. and Greenwood, R. (eds) (1992) *Jumbly Words and Rights where Wrongs should be: the Experience of Aphasia from the inside*. Kibworth: Far Communications.

Elias, A., Raven, R., Butcher. P. and Littlejohns, D.W. (1989) 'Speech therapy for psychogenic voice disorders: a survey of current practice and training', *British Journal of Disorders of Communication*, 24 (1): 61–76.

Enderby, P. (1992) 'Outcome measures in speech therapy: impairment, disability, handicap and distress', *Health Trends*, 24 (2): 61–4.

Evesham, M. (1987) 'Residential courses for stutterers combining technique and personal construct psychology', in C. Levy (ed.), *Stuttering Therapies: Practical Approaches*. London and Sydney: Croom Helm.

Fawcus, M. (ed.) (1991) *Voice Disorders and their Management*, 2nd edn. London, New York, Tokyo, Melbourne and Madras: Chapman and Hall.

Fawcus, M. (1992) *Group Encounters in Speech and Language Therapy*. Leicester: Far Communications.

Fawcus, R. (1991) 'Mutational disorders of voice' in M. Fawcus (ed.), *Voice Disorders and their Management*, 2nd edn. London, New York, Tokyo, Melbourne and Madras: Chapman and Hall.

Fransella, F. (1972) *Personal Change and Reconstruction*. London and New York: Academic Press.

Fransella, F. (1980) 'Teaching personal construct psychotherapy' in A.W. Landfield and L.M. Leitner (eds), *Personal Construct Psychology: Psychotherapy and Personality*. New York, Chichester, Brisbane and Toronto: John Wiley.

Fransella. F. (1981) 'Nature babbling to herself: the self characterization as a therapeutic tool', in H. Bonarius, R. Holland, S. Rosenberg (eds), *Personal Construct Psychology: Recent Advances in Theory and Practice*. London and Basingstoke: Macmillan Publishers Ltd.

Fransella, F. (1993) 'The construct of resistance in psychotherapy' in G. Dunnett and L.M. Leitner (eds), *Critical Issues in Personal Construct Theory*. Malabar, FL: Krieger.

Fransella, F. and Bannister, D. (1977) *A Manual for Repertory Grid Technique*. London: Academic Press.

Fransella, F. and Dalton, P. (1990) *Personal Construct Counselling in Action*. London: Sage.

Gordon, N. (1991) 'The relationship between language and behaviour', *Developmental Medicine and Child Neurology*, 33: 86–9.

Green, D. (1986) 'Impact on the self: head injury in adolescence', *Constructs*, 4 (1). Newsletter of the Centre for Personal Construct Psychology, London.

Greene, M. and Mathieson, L. (1989) *The Voice and its Disorders*, 5th edn. London: Whurr.

Hall, B. (1991) 'Attitudes of fourth and sixth graders towards peers with mild articulation disorders', *Language, Speech and Hearing Services in Schools*, 22 (1): 334–40.

Hammarberg, B. (1987) 'Pitch and quality characteristics of mutational voice disorders before and after therapy', *Folia Phoniatrica*, 39 (4): 204–16.

Hartman, J. and Landau, W. (1987) 'Comparison of formal language therapy with supportive counseling for aphasia due to acute vascular accident', *Archives of Neurology*, 44 (6): 646–9.

Hayhow, R. (1987) 'Personal construct therapy with children and their families', in C. Levy (ed.), *Stuttering Therapies: Practical Approaches*. London and Sydney: Croom Helm.

Hayhow, R. and Levy, C. (1989) *Working with Stuttering: a Personal Construct Therapy Approach*. Bicester: Winslow Press.

Henze, K.H. and Kiese, C. (1990) 'Phoniatrische Psychologie: Ein junges Tatigheitsfeld in der Klinischen Praxis', *Psychologische Rundschau*, 41 (3): 159–61.

Hinkle, D. (1965) 'The change of personal constructs from the viewpoint of a theory of construct implications', PhD dissertation, Ohio State University.

Hodkinson, E. (1991) 'Therapy and management of the dysphonic child', in M. Fawcus (ed.), *Voice Disorders and their Management*. London, New York, Tokyo, Melbourne and Madras: Chapman and Hall.

House, A. and Andrews, B. (1987) 'The psychiatric and social characteristics of patients with functional dysphonia', *Journal of Psychosomatic Research*, 31 (4): 483–90.

Howard, D. and Hatfield, F.M. (1987) *Aphasia Therapy: Historical and Contemporary Issues*. Hove and London: Erlbaum.

Ingham, R.J. and Onslow, M. (1985) 'Measurement and modification of speech naturalness during stuttering therapy', *Journal of Speech and Hearing Disorders*, 50: 261–81.

Insley, T. (1987) 'A personal view of stuttering therapy', in C. Levy (ed.), *Stuttering Therapies: Practical Approaches*. London, New York and Sydney: Croom Helm.

Jackson, S.R. (1988) 'Self-characterisation: dimensions of meaning', in F. Fransella and L. Thomas (eds), *Experimenting with Personal Construct Psychology*. London and New York: Routledge and Kegan Paul.

Jackson, S.R. and Bannister, D. (1985) 'Growing into self', in D. Bannister (ed.), *Issues and Approaches in Personal Construct Theory*. London: Academic Press.

Kalita, N.G. and Zverkova, I.V.C. (1985) 'Psychological analysis of a new method system for rehabilitation of communication speech function in aphasia', *Defektologiya*, 1: 3–10.

Kelly, G.A. (1955) *The Psychology of Personal Constructs*. New York: Norton.

Kelly, G.A. (1969) 'In whom confide: on whom depend for what', in B. Maher (ed.), *Clinical Psychology and Personality*. New York: Krieger.

Lockhart, M.S. and Robertson, A.W. (1977) 'Hypnosis and speech therapy as a combined therapeutic approach to the problem of stammering', *British Journal of Disorders of Communication*, 12: 97–108.

Mearns, D. (1993) 'The ending phase of counselling', in W. Dryden (ed.), *Questions and Answers on Counselling in Action*. London, Newbury Park and New Delhi: Sage.

Miller, C. (1990a) 'The music behind the words', *CST Bulletin*: 454.

Miller, C. (1990b) 'Counselling in speech therapy', *CST Bulletin*: 455.

Monast, S. and Burke, D. (1985) 'Sexuality of the adolescent with neurogenic communicative disorders', *International Journal of Adolescent Medicine and Health*, 1: 315–23.

Nadell, J. (1991) 'Towards an existential psychotherapy with the traumatically brain injured patient', *Cognitive Rehabilitation*, 9 (6): 8–13.

Neimeyer, R.A. (1986) 'Person construct therapy', in W. Dryden and W. Golden (eds), *Cognitive Behavioural Approaches to Psychotherapy*, London: Harper & Row.

Nichols, F. (1993) 'Family therapy with aphasics', paper presented at the British Aphasiology Society Study Day: Approaching Counselling in Aphasia. Bristol, April.

Noonan, E. (1983) *Counselling Young People*. Methuen.

Ravenette, A.T. (1977) 'Personal construct theory: an approach to the psychological investigation of children and young people', in D. Bannister (ed.), *New Perspectives in Personal Construct Theory*. London and New York: Academic Press.

Ravenette, A.T. (1980) 'The exploration of consciousness: personal construct intervention with children', in A.W. Landfield and L.M. Leitner (eds), *Personal Construct Psychology: Psychotherapy and Personality*. New York, Chichester, Brisbane and Toronto: John Wiley.

Ravanette, A.T. (1987) 'Personal construct psychology and practitioners who work with children', paper prepared by The Centre for Personal Construct Psychology: London.

Ravenette, A.T. (1989) 'Who are you? A structure for exploring the sense of self'. Unpublished occasional paper.

Ravenette, A.T. (1990) 'A drawing and its opposite'. Unpublished occasional paper.

Rinaldi, W. (1991) 'The meaning of moderate learning difficulties at secondary school age'. *CSLT Bulletin*: ISSN 0953-6086.

Ritchie, D. (1960) *Stroke: A Diary of Recovery*. London: Faber and Faber.

Rustin, L. (1987) 'The treatment of childhood dysfluency through active parental involvement', in L. Rustin, H. Purser and D. Rowley (eds), *Progress in the Treatment of Fluency Disorders*. London, New York and Philadelphia: Taylor Francis.

Rustin, L., Purser, H. and Rowley, D. (eds) (1987) *Progress in the Treatment of Fluency Disorders*. London, New York and Philadelphia: Taylor Francis.

Ryle, A. (1985) 'The dyad grid and psychotherapy research', in N. Beail (ed.), *Repertory Grid Technique and Personal Constructs*. London and Sydney: Croom Helm.

Salmon, P. (1976) 'Grid measures with child subjects', in P. Slater (ed.), *Explorations of Intrapersonal Space*. London and New York: John Wiley.

Shapiro, L.E. (1984) *The New Short-term Therapies for Children: a Guide for the Helping Professions and Parents*. New Jersey: Prentice-Hall.

Sheehan, J.G. (1975) 'Conflict theory and avoidance-reduction therapy', in J. Eisenson (ed.), *Stuttering: a Second Symposium*. New York: Harper and Row.

Snaith, P. (1981) *Clinical Neurosis*. Oxford: Oxford University Press.

Sparkes, C. (1993) 'The impact of language loss on marriage', *CSLT Bulletin*: 494.

Streit, N.B. (1988) 'Separation-individuation and speech and language development in the psychotherapy of an atypical child', *Adolescent Social Work Journal*, 5 (2): 84–101.

Webster, R.L. (1980) Evolution of a target-based behavioural therapy for stuttering', *Journal of Fluency Disorders*, 5: 303–20.

Wertz, R. (1988) 'Comparison of treatment with counseling is not a test of treatment for aphasia', *Archives of Neurology*, 45 (4): 371–2.

Williams S.E. and Freer, C.A. (1986) 'Aphasia: its effects on marital relationships', *Archives of Physical Medical Rehabilitation*, 67: 250–2.

Index